Book of Lists

DAVID WALLECHINSKY is the author of numerous books, including *Tyrants: The World's 20 Worst Living Dictators* and *The Twentieth Century: History with the Boring Parts Left Out*. He is also vice-president of the International Society of Olympic Historians.

AMY WALLACE is the co-author of five previous volumes of *The Book of Lists*, as well as several other popular books. She is also the author of *The Psychic Healing Book* and *Sorcerer's Apprentice: My Life With Carlos Castaneda*. She currently lives in Los Angeles, with her two cats, Hank and Bella.

Also in the series

The Little
Book of Lists

David Wallechinsky and Amy Wallace

CANONGATE

Edinburgh · New York · Melbourne

First published in Great Britain in 2006 by
Canongate Books Ltd, 14 High Street,
Edinburgh, EH1 1TE

2

The images used in the text come from the Japanese edition of
The Book of Lists, published by Shufunotomosha in 2006

British Library Cataloguing-in-Publication Data
A catalogue record for this book is available on request from
the British Library

1 84195 853 0 (10-digit ISBN)
978 1 84195 853 8 (13-digit ISBN)

Designed and Typeset by Cluny Sheeler

Printed and bound in Great Britain by Clays Ltd, St Ives plc

www.canongate.net

This book is dedicated to the memory
of our father, Irving Wallace, who was

I OF A KIND

Contents

Contributors

A.E.	Ann Elwood
A.W.	Amy Wallace
C.F.	Chris Fishel
C.O.M.	Carol Orsag-Madigan
D.B.	Danny Biederman
D.L.	Don Lessem
D.W.	David Wallechinsky
I.W.	Irving Wallace
J.BA.	James Barnett
K.P.	Karen Pedersen
R.A.	Randy Alfred
R.H.	Robert Hendrickson
R.J.F.	Rodger J. Fadness
R.S.	Ray Spangenburg

Lists without initials were written by A.W. and D.W.

11 Examples of Unusual Animal Mating Habits

1. Penguins

Penguins prefer to be 'married', but they suffer long separations due to their migratory habits. When reunited, a pair will stand breast to breast, heads thrown back, singing loudly, with outstretched flippers trembling. Two weeks after a pair is formed, their union is consummated. The male makes his intentions known by laying his head across his partner's stomach. They go on a long trek to find privacy, but the actual process of intercourse takes only three minutes. Neither penguin will mate again that year.

The male Adele penguin must select his mate from a colony of more than a million, and he indicates his choice by rolling a stone at the female's feet. (Stones are scarce at mating time because many are needed to build walls around nests. It becomes commonplace for penguins to steal them from one another.) If she accepts this gift, they stand belly to belly and sing a mating song.

2. Hippopotami

Hippos have their own form of aromatherapy. Hippos attract mates by marking territory, urinating and defecating at the same time. Then, an enamoured hippo will twirl its tail like a propeller to spread this delicious slop in every direction. This attracts lovers, and a pair will begin foreplay, which consists of playing by splashing around in the water before settling down to business.

3. The Male Uganda Kob

Exhaustion is the frequent fate of the male Uganda kob, an African antelope. Like many species of birds and mammals, the kob roams in a social group until the mating season, when the dominant male establishes a mating territory, or lek. But the females decide which territory they wish to enter and then pick the male they think most attractive. He then mates with all the females until he is too weak to continue (usually due to lack of food) and is replaced by another.

4. Squid

Squid begin mating with a circling nuptial dance. Teams of squid revolve around across a 'spawning bed' 200 metres in diameter. At daybreak they begin having sex and continue all day long – they only take a break so the female can drive down and deposit eggs. When she returns to the circle, the two go at it again. As twilight falls, the pair go offshore to eat and rest. At the first sign of sunlight, they return to their spot and do it all over again. This routine can last up to two weeks, ensuring a healthy population of squid.

5. Porcupines

The answer to one of our oldest jokes: 'How do porcupines do it?' 'Veeery carefully!' is not quite true. The truth is more bizarre than dangerous. Females are only receptive for a few hours a year. As summer approaches, young females become nervous and very excited. Next, they go off their food, and stick close by the males and mope. Meanwhile the male becomes aggressive with other males, and begins a period of carefully sniffing every place the female of his choice urinates, smelling her all over. This is a tremendous aphrodisiac. While she is sulking by his side, he begins to 'sing'.

When he is ready to make love, the female runs away if she's not ready. If she is in the mood, they both rear up and face each other, belly-to-belly. Then, males spray their ladies with a tremendous stream of urine, soaking their loved one from head to foot – the stream can shoot as far as 7 feet.

If they're not ready, females respond by 1) objecting verbally 2) hitting with front paws like boxers 3) trying to bite 4) shaking off the urine. When ready, they accept the bath. This routine can go on for weeks. Six months after the beginning of courtship, the female will accept any male she has been close to. The spines and quills of both go relaxed and flat, and the male enters from behind. Mating continues until the male is worn out. Every time he tries to stop, the female wants to continue. If he has given up, she chooses another partner, only now *she* acts out the male role. To 'cool off', females engage in the same courtship series, step-by-step, in reverse order.

It is advised never to stand close to a cage that contains courting porcupines.

6. Geese

Two male geese may form a homosexual bond and prefer each other's company to any female's. Sometimes, however, a female may interpose herself between them during such a courtship, and be quickly fertilised. They will accept her, and weeks later the happy family of three can be seen attending to its tiny newborn goslings.

7. White-fronted parrots

These birds, native to Mexico and Central America, are believed to be the only species besides humans to kiss. Before actually mating, male and female will lock their beaks and gently flick their tongues together. If kissing is satisfying for both parties, the male boldly takes the next step, by regurgitating his food for his girlfriend, to show his love. White-fronted parrots also share parenting, unlike many other species. When the female lays her one egg, both parents take turns incubating it. When the baby hatches, the couple feed and care for their offspring together.

8. Grasshoppers

Why are grasshoppers so noisy? It's because they're singing to woo their partners. They have as many as 400 distinct songs, which they sing during their courtship and mating cycles. Some males have a different song for each distinct mating period – for example, there may be a flirting song, then a mating song.

9. Seagulls

Lesbian mating is practised by between 8% and 14% of the seagulls on the Santa Barbara islands, off the California coast. Lesbian gulls go through all the motions of mating, and they lay sterile eggs. Homosexual behaviour is also known in geese, ostriches, cichlid fish, squid, rats and monkeys.

10. Red-sided Garter Snakes

These snakes are small and poisonous, and live in Canada and the Northwestern United States. Their highly unusual mating takes place during an enormous orgy. Twenty-five thousand snakes slither together in a large den, eager to copulate. In that pile, one female may have as many as 100 males vying for her. These 'nesting balls' grow as large as two feet high. Now and then a female is crushed under the heavy mound – and the males are so randy that they continue to copulate, becoming the only necrophiliac snakes!

11. Lynx Spiders

When a male lynx spider feels the urge, he will capture his beauty in his web and wrap her in silk. Offering her this elegant meal (the silken web) is his way of wooing. When the mood is right, the female, distracted by her feast, will allow her suitor to mount her and begin mating. Oblivious, she ignores him and enjoys her supper.

23 Actors Who Turned Down Great Roles

1. Marlon Brando

Turned down the role of Frankie, the musician-junkie, in *The Man with the Golden Arm* (1955). Frank Sinatra got the part and re-established his career with an electrifying performance.

2. James Cagney

Turned down the role of Alfred P. Doolittle in *My Fair Lady* (1964). The role went to Stanley Holloway. Cagney was offered $1 million but did not want to come out of retirement.

3. Montgomery Clift

Expressed enthusiasm for the role of the young writer in *Sunset Boulevard* (1950), but later turned it down, claiming that his audience would not accept his playing love scenes with a woman who was 35 years older. William Holden starred with Gloria Swanson in the widely acclaimed film.

4. Sean Connery

Long a fan-favourite to play Gandalf, the venerable wizard from J.R.R. Tolkien's *Lord of the Rings* trilogy, the star turned the role down because he did not want to spend 18 months filming in New Zealand. Sir Ian McKellan eventually played the role to wide acclaim in the film trilogy. After the massive success of the first film, *The Fellowship of the Ring*, Connery said, 'I had never read Tolkien, and the script when they sent it to me, I didn't understand . . . bobbits, hobbits . . . I will see it.'

5. Bette Davis

Turned down the role of Scarlett O'Hara in *Gone with the Wind* (1939). The role went to Vivien Leigh. Davis thought that her co-star was going to be Errol Flynn, with whom she refused to work.

6. Kirk Douglas

Turned down the role of Kid Shelleen in *Cat Ballou* (1965). The role won an Academy Award for Lee Marvin. Douglas's agent convinced him not to accept the comedic role of the drunken gunfighter.

7. W.C. Fields

Could have played the title role in *The Wizard of Oz* (1939). The part was written for Fields, who would have played the wizard as a cynical con man. But he turned down the part, purportedly because he wanted $100,000 and MGM only offered him $75,000. However, a letter signed by Fields's agent asserts that Fields rejected the offer in order to devote all his time to writing *You Can't Cheat an Honest Man*. Frank Morgan ended up playing the wizard.

8. Jane Fonda

Turned down *Bonnie and Clyde* (1967). The role of Bonnie Parker went to Faye Dunaway. Fonda, living in France at the time, did not want to move to the United States for the role.

9. Cary Grant

Producers Albert Broccoli and Harry Saltzman, who had bought the film rights to Ian Fleming's James Bond novels, originally approached Cary Grant about playing 007. Grant declined because he did not want to become involved in a film series. Instead, Sean Connery was cast as Bond, starting with *Dr No* (1962). Fleming's comment on this casting choice: 'He's not exactly what I had in mind.'

10–11. Gene Hackman and Michelle Pfeiffer

Orion Pictures acquired the film rights to *Silence of the Lambs* in 1988 because Gene Hackman had expressed an interest in directing and writing the screenplay for it. He would also star as serial killer Hannibal Lecter. By mid-1989, Hackman had dropped out of the project. Jonathan Demme took over as director and offered the female lead of FBI agent-in-training Clarice Starling to Michelle Pfeiffer, with whom he had worked in *Married to the Mob* (1988). Pfeiffer felt the film was too dark and decided not to be in it. When *Silence of the Lambs* was made in 1990, the lead roles were played by Anthony

Hopkins and Jodie Foster. Both won Academy Awards for their performances.

12. Alan Ladd
Turned down the role of Jett Rink in *Giant* (1956). The role went to James Dean. Ladd felt he was too old for the part.

13. Hedy Lamarr
Turned down the role of Ilsa in *Casablanca* (1942). Ingrid Bergman took over and, with Bogart, made film history. Lamarr had not wanted to work with an unfinished script.

14. Burt Lancaster
Turned down the lead in *Ben-Hur* (1959). The role of Judah Ben-Hur went to Charlton Heston, who won an Academy Award and added another hit to his career of spectacular blockbusters.

15. Myrna Loy

Turned down the lead (Ellie Andrews) opposite Clark Gable (Peter Warne) in *It Happened One Night* (1934). The role led to an Academy Award for Claudette Colbert. A previous film set on a bus had just failed, and Loy thought the film would not have a chance.

16. Michael Madsen

After his terrifyingly menacing performance in *Reservoir Dogs* (1992), Michael Madsen was offered the role of Vincent Vega in Quentin Tarantino's next film as director, *Pulp Fiction* (1994). He turned it down because he was involved in the making of *Wyatt Earp* (1994) in which he plays Virgil Earp. *Pulp Fiction* was an enormous success with audiences and critics. *Wyatt Earp* wasn't. John Travolta, who played Vincent Vega, found his career on the up and up while Madsen found himself playing parts in a series of B pictures. 'I wanted to take a walk down to the OK Corral,' Madsen has been quoted as saying. 'If I'd known how long a walk it was gonna be, I'd have taken a cab.'

17–18. Ewan McGregor and Will Smith

Both of these stars turned down the role of Neo in the block-buster science-fiction epic *The Matrix*, which eventually went to Keanu Reeves. McGregor starred as the young Obi-Wan Kenobi in *Star Wars: The Phantom Menace* instead, while Smith – who went on to star in the film version of Isaac Asimov's *I, Robot* – admitted, 'I watched Keanu's performance – and very rarely do I say this – but I would have messed it up. I would have absolutely messed up *The Matrix*. At that point I wasn't smart enough as an actor to let the movie be.'

19. Steve McQueen

When Paul Newman asked McQueen to star opposite him in *Butch Cassidy and the Sundance Kid* (1969), McQueen insisted on top billing. When his demand was turned down, McQueen refused to appear in the film. Robert Redford played Sundance and became the most sought-after star of the 1970s. McQueen turned down the lead role of Popeye Doyle in *The French Connection* (1971) because he felt the part was too similar to the tough cop he had played in *Bullitt* (1969).

Gene Hackman got the part and won an Oscar for it. Finally, when director Francis Ford Coppola offered McQueen the starring role of Captain Willard in *Apocalypse Now* (1979), McQueen declined because he did not want to spend 16 weeks – Coppolla's original shooting schedule – on location in the Philippine jungles, away from his new bride, Ali MacGraw. Martin Sheen, who accepted the role, ended up spending a year and a half on location and almost died from a massive heart attack during the filming. Nonetheless, he turned in an electrifying performance.

20. Gregory Peck

The producer of *High Noon* (1952), Stanley Kramer, originally offered the role of Will Kane, the retiring marshal who stays in town to confront the gunmen out to kill him, to Gregory Peck. Peck turned it down because he thought it was too similar to the part of Jimmy Ringo, an aging gunslinger haunted by his own reputation, which he had played in *The Gunfighter* (1950). Several other actors, including Montgomery Clift, Charlton Heston and Marlon Brando were approached before Gary Cooper was signed to play Kane. He went on to win an Oscar for Best Actor for his performance.

21. George Raft

Turned down the main roles in *High Sierra* (1941), *The Maltese Falcon* (1941) and *Casablanca* (1942), which became three of Humphrey Bogart's most famous roles. Raft rejected the Sam Spade role in *The Maltese Falcon* because he did not want to work with director John Huston, an unknown at that time.

22. Robert Redford

Turned down the role of Ben Braddock in *The Graduate* (1967). The role made an instant star of Dustin Hoffman. Redford thought he could not project the right amount of naiveté.

23. Eva Marie Saint

Known for her selectivity in choosing roles, she erred when she turned down the central role in *The Three Faces of Eve*

(1957) after reading an early version of the script. Joanne Woodward won an Oscar for her performance in the film.

— R.S. & C.F.

8 Memorable Lines Erroneously Attributed to Film Stars

1. 'Smile when you say that, pardner.'

What Gary Cooper actually said to Walter Huston in *The Virginian* (1929) was, 'If you want to call me that, smile.'

2. 'Me Tarzan, you Jane.'

Johnny Weismuller's first Tarzan role was in *Tarzan, the Ape Man* (1932). He introduced himself to co-star Maureen O'Sullivan by thumping his chest and announcing, 'Tarzan'. He then gingerly tapped *her* chest and said, 'Jane'.

3. 'You dirty rat.'

In fact, James Cagney never uttered this line in any of his roles as a hard-boiled gangster. It has often been used by impersonators, however, to typify Cagney's tough-guy image.

4. 'Come with me to the Casbah.'

Charles Boyer cast seductive glances at Hedy Lamarr throughout *Algiers* (1938), but he never did make this suggestion. Delivered with a French accent, the line appeals to many Boyer imitators who enjoy saying, 'Come weez mee . . .'

5. 'Why don't you come up and see me sometime?'

Cary Grant found himself the recipient of Mae West's lusty invitation, 'Why don't you come up sometime and see me?' in *She Done Him Wrong* (1933).

6. 'Play it again, Sam.'

In *Casablanca* (1942) Ingrid Bergman dropped in unexpectedly at old lover Humphrey Bogart's nightclub, where she asked the piano player to 'Play it, Sam', referring to the song

'As Time Goes By'. Although Bogart's character was shocked at hearing the song that reminded him so painfully of his lost love, he also made Sam play it again – but the words he used were, 'You played it for her, you can play it for me . . . play it.'

7. 'Judy, Judy, Judy.'

Cary Grant has never exclaimed this line in any film, but imitators often use it to display their Cary Grant-like accents.

8. 'I want to be alone.'

In 1955, retired film star Greta Garbo – despairing of ever being free of publicity – said, 'I want to be let alone.' The melodramatic misinterpretation, however, is the way most people have heard and quoted it.

– K.P.

17 Movie Stars and How They Were Discovered

1. Fatty Arbuckle

The hefty comedian got his first break due to a blocked drain. Working as a plumber's assistant, he was summoned to unclog Mack Sennett's pipes in 1913 and the producer immediately offered Arbuckle a job in his Keystone Kops comedies.

2. Richard Arlen

He was working as a film lab runner at Paramount Studios in 1922 when he was struck by a company car and hospitalised with a broken leg. Studio executives took notice and offered him a chance to act.

3. Walter Brennan

He got his start in Hollywood in 1932 when he did a voiceover for a donkey. The actor volunteered to help a film director who was having difficulty getting the animal to bray on cue.

4. Ellen Burstyn

She was cast in her first major role in *Tropic of Cancer* (1969) on the basis of a political speech that director Joseph Strick heard her delivering.

5. Gary Cooper

Working as a stunt man, he was noticed by director Henry King on the set of *The Winning of Barbara Worth* at Samuel Goldwyn Studios in 1926.

6. Errol Flynn

He was discovered by Cinesound Studios casting director John Warwick in Sydney, Australia, in 1932. Warwick found some amateur footage of Flynn taken in 1930 by Dr Herman

F. Erben, a filmmaker and tropical-disease specialist who had chartered navigator Flynn's schooner for a tour of New Guinea headhunter territory.

7. Rock Hudson

Hudson, whose original name was Roy Fitzgerald, was working as a truck driver for the Budget Pack Company in 1954 when another driver offered to arrange a meeting between Fitzgerald and agent Henry Willson. In spite of Fitzgerald's professed lack of faith in his acting abilities, Willson took the aspiring actor under his wing, changed his name to Rock Hudson, and launched his career.

8. Janet Leigh

She was a psychology student when MGM star Norma Shearer happened to see a photo of her at a ski lodge in northern California where her parents were employed. Shearer took it to the studio with the result that Leigh was given a role in *The Romance of Rosy Ridge* (1947).

9. Gina Lollobrigida

An art student in Rome, she was stopped on the street by director Mario Costa. She let loose a torrent of abuse about men who accost defenceless girls and only when she paused for breath was he able to explain that he wanted to screentest her for *Elisir d'Amore* (1946). She won the part.

10. Carole Lombard

She met director Allan Dwan in Los Angeles in the spring of 1921. Dwan watched 12-year-old Carole – then tomboy Jane Alice Peters – playing baseball outside the home of his friends Al and Rita Kaufman.

11. Ida Lupino

She was introduced to director Allan Dwan in England in 1933, while Dwan was casting a film, *Her First Affair*. Forty-one-year-old Connie Emerald was trying out for a part, but Dwan found Connie's 15-year-old daughter Ida better suited for the role.

12. Mae Marsh

One of the first actresses to achieve screen stardom without previous stage experience, Marsh was a 17-year-old salesgirl when she stopped by the Biograph Studios to see her sister, Marguerite Loveridge. She was spotted by director D.W. Griffith, who was having problems because none of his contract players was willing to play the lead in *Man's Genesis* (1912) with bared legs. Marsh had no such inhibitions when Griffith offered her the part.

13. Ryan O'Neal

He was befriended by actor Richard Egan in 1962 at the gymnasium where both Egan and O'Neal worked out. 'It was just a matter of Ryan himself being so impressive,' said Egan.

14. Telly Savalas

He was teaching adult-education classes in Garden City, New Jersey, when an agent asked him if he knew an actor who could speak with a European accent. He tried out himself and landed a part in Armstrong Circle Theater on television.

15. Charlize Theron

The South African-born actress studied dance and modelled in Milan and New York before heading to Los Angeles to pursue her dream of acting. After several difficult months in LA, Theron's discovery came in a Hollywood Boulevard bank. When a teller refused to cash an out-of-town cheque for her, she threw an enormous tantrum which caught the attention of veteran talent manager John Crosby, who happened to be standing nearby. Crosby handed her his business card as she was being thrown out of the bank. After signing with Crosby, Theron landed a star-making role as a sexy assassin in 1996's *2 Days in the Valley*. She ended her association with Crosby in 1997, and has starred in such films as *The Cider House Rules*, *The Italian Job* and *Monster*, which won Theron the Best Actress in a Leading Role Oscar in 2004 for her portrayal of serial killer Aileen Wuornos.

16. Lana Turner

She was observed in Currie's Ice Cream Parlor across the street from Hollywood High School in January 1936. Billy

Wilkerson, editor of the *Hollywood Reporter*, approached her while she was drinking a Coke.

17. John Wayne

He was spotted by director Raoul Walsh at Hollywood's Fox lot in 1928. Walsh was on his way to the administration building when he noticed Wayne – then Marion Morrison, a studio prop man – loading furniture from a warehouse onto a truck.

– D.B. & C.F.

Stephen King's 6 Scariest Scenes Ever Captured on Film

The author of such bestselling novels of terror as *Carrie*, *Salem's Lot*, *Night Shift*, *The Stand*, *The Shining*, *The Dead Zone* and *Fire Starter*, Stephen King is the modern master of the macabre. His style is highly visual, revealing an early and strong influence by film. Although he has probably instilled more fear in the hearts of readers than any other contemporary writer, he, too, has experienced chilling moments in the darkness of the cinema.

1. *Wait Until Dark* (1967, Terence Young)

The moment near the conclusion, when [Alan] Arkin jumps out at Audrey Hepburn, is a real scare.

2. *Carrie* (1976, Brian De Palma)

The dream sequence at the end, when Sissy Spacek thrusts her hand out of the ground and grabs Amy Irving. I knew it was coming and I still felt as if I'd swallowed a snowcone whole.

3. *I Bury the Living* (1958, Albert Band)

In this almost-forgotten movie, there is a chilling sequence when [Richard] Boone begins to maniacally remove the black pins in the filled graveyard plots and to replace them with white pins.

4. *The Texas Chainsaw Massacre* (1974, Tobe Hooper)

The moment when the corpse seems to leap out of the freezer like a hideous jack-in-the-box.

5. *Night of the Living Dead* (1968, George Romero)

The scene where the little girl stabs her mother to death with a garden trowel in the cellar . . . 'Mother, please, I can do it myself.'

6. *Psycho* (1960, Alfred Hitchcock)

The shower scene, of course.

Source: Gabe Essoe, *The Book of Movie Lists* (Westport Arlington House, 1981)

7 Great Sausage Events

1. Comic Sausage

Epicharmus, a Greek dramatist who lived during the golden age of Sophocles and Aeschylus, wrote a comedy titled *Orya* ('The Sausage') around 500BC. Because the play exists today only as a fragment, we will never know exactly what the Greeks thought was funny about sausage.

2. Heathen Sausage

The ancient Romans were so fond of pork sausage spiced with pine nuts and pepper that the dish became a staple of the annual Lupercalian and Floralian festivals. Since these pagan celebrations usually degenerated into orgiastic rites, the early Christians looked upon them with disapproval. When Constantine the Great, a Christian, became emperor in AD324, he outlawed the production and consumption of the sinful sausage. But the Romans refused to cooperate and developed a flourishing black market in sausage. They continued to eat the bootlegged delicacies throughout the reigns of several Christian emperors until the ban was finally lifted.

3. Fatal Sausage

At a simple peasant meal in Wildbad, Germany, in 1793, 13 people shared a single sausage. Within hours they became seriously ill, and six of them died. Their disease became known as botulism – a word coined from the Latin for sausage, botulus. The powerfully toxic bacteria *Clostridium botulinum* inside the sausage could have been easily killed by boiling it for two minutes. Once in the body, botulism toxins attack the nervous system, causing paralysis of all muscles, which brings on death by suffocation.

4. Human Sausage

Adolph Luetgert, a Chicago sausage maker, was so fond of entertaining his mistresses that he had a bed installed in his factory. Louisa Luetgert was aware of her husband's infidelities and, in 1897, their marriage took a dramatic turn for the worse. Louisa subsequently disappeared, and when the police arrived to search Luetgert's factory, they found human teeth and bones – as well as two gold rings engraved 'L.L.' – at the bottom of a sausage vat. During his well-publicised trial, Luetgert maintained his innocence, but he was convicted of murder and spent the rest of his life in prison.

5. Muckraking Sausage

Upton Sinclair's novel *The Jungle*, an exposé of conditions in the Chicago stockyards and meat industry, contained shocking descriptions: 'There was never the least attention paid to what was cut up for sausage . . . there would be meat stored in great piles . . . thousands of rats would race about on it . . . these rats were nuisances, and the packers would put poisoned bread out for them; they would die, and then rats, bread and meat would go into the hoppers together.' Americans were deeply alarmed by the filth described, and in the same year the book was published, Congress passed the Pure Food and Drug Act of 1906.

6.   Insolent Sausage

In October 1981, Joseph Guillou, an engineer on the Moroccan tanker *Al Ghassani*, was arrested, fined £50, and sentenced to two years in jail for insulting Morocco's King Hassan. Guillou's offence was hanging a sausage on the hook normally reserved for a portrait of the monarch. A sausage, said Guillou, was 'more useful than a picture of the king'.

7.   Victim Sausage

During home games at Miller Park, the Milwaukee Brewers baseball team holds 'sausage races' in which people costumed as different types of sausages run around the park between innings. During a game on July 9, 2003, as the runners passed the visiting team's dugout, Randall Simon, the first baseman for the Pittsburgh Pirates, struck the Italian sausage, Mandy Block, with his bat, knocking her to the ground. After the game, Simon was handcuffed by Milwaukee County sheriff's deputies, taken to a police station, and fined $432 for disorderly conduct. The sausage whacking was broadcast repeatedly, but Block ignored the controversy, accepting Simon's apology. When he returned to Miller Park later in the season, Simon bought Italian sausages for a section of fans. Block was recognised by the National Hot Dog and Sausage Council with a certificate of bravery. 'I'm proud of it,' Block said. 'I didn't even know there was a hot dog council.'

– K.P.

Average Erect Penis Lengths for 10 Species

Animal	Average Erect Penis Length
1. Humpback whale	10 ft
2. Elephant	5–6 ft
3. Bull	3 ft
4. Stallion	2 ft 6 in.

5. Rhinoceros   2 ft
6. Pig   18–20 in.
7. Man   6 in.
8. Gorilla   2 in.
9. Cat   ¾ in.
10. Mosquito $^1/_{100}$ in.

Source: Leigh Rutledge, *The Gay Book of Lists* (Boston: Alyson Publications, 1987)

15 Actors Who Became Politicians

1. Helen Gahagan Douglas

A Broadway star, Gahagan moved to Hollywood after marrying film actor Melvyn Douglas. Her brief movie career was highlighted by her leading role in the cult classic *She* (1935). After several years' involvement in Democratic Party politics, she was elected to Congress in 1944 and served three terms. Gahagan Douglas ran for the US Senate in California in 1950, facing up-and-coming right-winger Richard Nixon. Nixon scared voters by calling her 'red hot' and 'pink right down to her underwear' and by insinuating that she had slept with President Truman. Nixon won the election and went on to further political success. Gahagan Douglas never ran for office again.

2. Clint Eastwood

In 1986, the star by then of such films as *A Fistful of Dollars* (1964), *Dirty Harry* (1971) and *Sudden Impact* (1983), Eastwood took time off from his film career to serve two years as mayor of Carmel, California (population 4,800). Elected on a pro-development platform in 1986, Eastwood nonetheless stopped greedy developers from buying the 22-acre Mission Ranch by buying it himself for $5 million.

3. Joseph Estrada

Known as the 'Filipino Ronald Reagan' because he starred in so many B-movies, Estrada built his reputation by playing the role of the common man fighting the system. Elected mayor of San Juan, a suburb of Manila, Estrada moved on to become the only senator without a college degree. In 1992 he was elected vice-president of the Philippines. Estrada was elected president of the Philippines in 1998. In 2000, he was impeached by the Philippine Congress on charges of corruption and bribery. He resigned on January 20, 2001, in the face of a bloodless 'people's revolt'. He has since served time in prison for perjury.

4. Fred Grandy

Although he has appeared on Broadway as well as in movies, Grandy, a Harvard graduate, is best known for his portrayal of Gopher in the TV series *The Love Boat* (1977–86). In 1986 he returned to his earlier interest in politics, winning election from Sioux City, Iowa, to the US House of Representatives. A Republican, Grandy describes himself as a 'knee-jerk moderate'.

5. Glenda Jackson

Jackson won two Academy Awards for her performances in *Women in Love* (1970) and *A Touch of Class* (1972). Running as a Labour Party candidate, the bricklayer's daughter won election to Parliament in 1992 in the Hampstead and Highgate constituencies of north London and has since had a committed career as an MP.

6. Ben Jones

Best known for his portrayal of the mechanic Cooter Davenport in *The Dukes of Hazzard*, Jones, a Georgia Democrat, won election to the US Congress in 1988. He was re-elected in 1990, but in 1992 he was defeated in the Democratic Party primary.

7. Sheila Kuehl

Kuehl played Zelda Gilroy in the TV series *The Many Loves of Dobie Gillis* from 1959 to 1963. After the series ended she went to law school and became an attorney specialising in feminist issues. In 1994 she was elected speaker pro tem of the California State Assembly, the first woman to hold that position. In 2000 she was elected to the State Senate. Kuehl was the first openly gay or lesbian politician to be elected to the California legislature.

8. Melina Mercouri

The star of *Never on Sunday* (1959), Mercouri entered Greek politics when democracy was restored in 1974. A member of the Pan-Hellenic Socialist movement, she was elected to Parliament in 1977 and has represented the working-class district of Piraeus ever since. She served as minister of culture from 1981 to 1990. In 1990 she ran for mayor of Athens but was defeated.

9. Alessandra Mussolini

No one was surprised or upset when the beautiful niece of actress Sophia Loren became a film actress herself, appearing in such films as *White Sister* (1973) and *A Special Day* (1977). But she did cause a stir when, at the age of 30, she followed in the footsteps of her grandfather, dictator Benito Mussolini, by entering politics. In 1992 she was elected to Parliament as the representative of the neo-Fascist party from Naples.

10. N.T. Rama Rao

Known as the 'Saffron Caesar' because he usually appeared in an orange costume, Rama Rao, the star of more than 300 Indian films, capitalised on his widespread popularity to enter politics. He rose to become chief minister of Andhra Pradesh state. After leaving office, he remained the leader of the Telegu Desam Party, and in 1991, at the age of 69, he was arrested in the midst of a hunger strike to protest at an attack on his house by supporters of the ruling Congress Party.

11. Ronald Reagan

Reagan was a movie actor, a president of the Screen Actors' Guild, and a Democrat-turned-Republican. When he announced that he planned to run for governor of California in 1966, studio head Jack Warner commented, 'No, no, no! Jimmy Stewart for governor, Ronald Reagan for best friend.' When he won the election, Reagan was asked what he planned to do when he took office. 'I don't know,' he replied, 'I've never played a governor.' Reagan was re-elected in 1970 and later served two terms as President of the United States (1981–89). Nevertheless, he never lost his basic actor's mentality. At the 1987 economic summit in Venice, Reagan startled the leaders of the world's industrial nations by showing up with cue cards, not just for important meetings, but even at an informal cocktail party.

12. Arnold Schwarzenegger

The bodybuilder-turned-actor rose to stardom in such films as *Conan the Barbarian* (1982) and *The Terminator* (1984). By the end of the 1980s, he was Hollywood's top action hero.

After he married into the Kennedy clan (his wife, broadcast journalist Maria Shriver, is the daughter of Eunice Kennedy Shriver), speculation grew about a possible political career. He saw his chance in 2003, when Republicans launched a drive to recall California's Democratic Governor Gray Davis from office. In true Hollywood fashion, Schwarzenegger announced his candidacy on August 7, 2003, to Jay Leno on *The Tonight Show*. Two months later, California voters chose to oust Davis and replace him with Schwarzenegger.

13. Ilona Staller

Hungarian-born pornographic film star Ilona Staller, better known by her stage name, Cicciolina, was elected to the Italian Parliament in 1987. A member of the Radical Party and the Party of Love, Staller represented her Rome constituency until she retired in 1992.

14. Fred Thompson

A veteran character actor, Thompson had prominent roles in the movies *The Hunt for Red October* (1990) and *In the Line of*

Fire (1993). A Republican from Tennessee, he was elected to the US Senate in 1994. In the autumn of 2002 Thompson joined the cast of the NBC series *Law and Order*, becoming the first serving US senator with a regular television acting job. He left the Senate when his term ended in January of 2003.

15. Jesse Ventura

Jesse 'The Body' Ventura first emerged as a star in the World Wrestling Federation. He parlayed that fame into a movie career, appearing with Arnold Schwarzenegger in *Predator* (1987) and with Sylvester Stallone in *Demolition Man* (1993). In 1998 he was elected Governor of Minnesota as the candidate of the upstart Reform Party. He drew fire from critics for appearing as a TV commentator for the short-lived XFL (Extreme Football League) and being a celebrity referee at a WWF event while still in office. He served one term, choosing not to run for re-election in 2002.

— D.W. & C.F.

29 Activities and the Calories They Consume

Activity	Calories per hour
1. Making mountains out of molehills	500
2. Running around in circles	350
3. Wading through paperwork	300
4. Pushing your luck	250
5. Eating crow	225
6. Flying off the handle	225
7. Jumping on the bandwagon	200
8. Spinning your wheels	175
9. Adding fuel to the fire	150
10. Beating your head against the wall	150
11. Climbing the walls	150
12. Jogging your memory	125
13. Beating your own drum	100

14.	Dragging your heels	100
15.	Jumping to conclusions	100
16.	Beating around the bush	75
17.	Bending over backwards	75
18.	Grasping at straws	75
19.	Pulling out the stops	75
20.	Turning the other cheek	75
21.	Fishing for compliments	50
22.	Hitting the nail on the head	50
23.	Pouring salt on a wound	50
24.	Swallowing your pride	50
25.	Throwing your weight around (depending on your weight)	50–300
26.	Passing the buck	25
27.	Tooting your own horn	25
28.	Balancing the books	23
29.	Wrapping it up at day's end	12

Source: *Bulletin*, Columbus Industrial Association, July 11, 1977

7 Extinct Animals That Are No Longer Extinct

1. Cahow

This ocean-wandering bird nested exclusively on the islets of Bermuda. Also known as the Bermuda petrel, the last of the cahows was believed to have been killed during the famine of 1615, when British colonists built cook-fires into which the unwary cahows flew by the thousand. On January 8, 1951, the cahow was rediscovered by Bermuda's conservation officer, David Wingate. Under his protection, the existing 18 birds were encouraged to breed, and now number more than 150.

2. Dibbler

A marsupial mouse, the dibbler was listed as extinct in 1884. In 1967 an Australian naturalist hoping to trap live honey possums, caught instead a pair of dibblers. The female of the captured pair soon produced a litter of eight, and they were then bred in captivity.

3. Dwarf Lemur

The last known dwarf lemur was reported in 1875, and was regarded as extinct. Then in 1966 the small tree-dwelling marsupial was once again seen, near the city of Mananara, Madagascar.

4. Mountain Pygmy Possum

This small marsupial was considered to have been extinct for 20,000 years until Dr Kenneth Shortman caught one in the kitchen of his skiing lodge, Mount Hothan, in southeast Australia in 1966. Three more of the tiny possums were discovered in 1970.

5–6. Tarpan and Aurochs

A primeval forest horse of central Asia and long extinct, the tarpan was recreated by brothers Lutz and Heinz Heck, curators of the Berlin and Munich zoos, respectively. By selective crossbreeding of Polish primitive horses with Swedish Gotlands, Icelandic ponies and Polish Konik mares, they created a strain of wild horse identical in appearance to what we know of the mouse-gray tarpan. The first colt was born on May 22, 1933. By this same method, the aurochs, a European wild ox which died out in Poland in 1627, has also been duplicated.

7. White-winged Guan

A flower-eating South American bird, the guan was thought extinct for a century until sighted in September of 1977. An American ornithologist and his Peruvian associate located four of the pheasant-sized birds in remote northwestern Peru.

— D.L.

5 Pieces of Advice on How to Survive an Encounter With a Bear

The following situations may occur anywhere in bear country. This recommended behaviour is generally advised, but is no guarantee of averting a mishap. Above all, remain calm and give the bear the opportunity to learn that your intentions are not hostile.

1. Never Run

Do not run. Bears can run faster than 30 miles (50 kilometres) per hour – even faster than Olympic sprinters. Running can elicit a chase response from otherwise nonaggressive bears.

2. An Unaware Bear

If the bear is unaware of you, detour quickly and quietly away from it. Give the bear plenty of room, allowing it to continue undisturbed.

3. An Aware Bear

If the bear is aware of you but has not acted aggressively, back away slowly, talking in a calm, firm voice while slowly waving your arms. Bears that stand up on their hind legs are usually just trying to identify you, and are not threatening.

4. An Approaching Bear

Do not run; do not drop your pack. A pack can help protect your body in case of an attack. To drop a pack may encourage the bear to approach people for food. Bears occasionally make 'bluff charges', sometimes coming to within ten feet of a person before stopping or veering off. Stand still until the bear stops and has moved away, then slowly back off. Climbing trees will not protect you from black bears, and may not provide protection from grizzlies.

5. If a Bear Touches You

If a grizzly bear does actually make contact with you, curl up in a ball, protecting your stomach and neck, and play dead. If the attack is prolonged, however, change tactics and fight back vigorously. If it is a black bear, do not play dead; fight back.

Source: Denali National Park and Preserve, Denali Park, Alaska

22 Memorable Kisses

1. The Kiss of Life

It was a kiss from God that infused the 'spirit of life' into man, according to the account of Genesis (2:7). God is said to have formed Adam from slime and dust and then breathed a rational soul into him. This concept of divine insufflation, which surfaces frequently in religious teachings, is often viewed through the kiss metaphor.

2. The Betrayal Kiss of Judas (c. AD29)

As told in the New Testament, Judas Iscariot used the kiss as a tool of betrayal around AD29, when he embraced Jesus Christ in the Garden of Gethsemane. Jewish leaders under the high priest Caiaphas had paid Judas 30 pieces of silver to identify Jesus. With a kiss, Judas singled him out. Jesus was arrested; charged with blasphemy and condemned to death.

3. The Kiss That Awakened Sleeping Beauty (17th century)

In the classic fairy tale 'Sleeping Beauty', it is with a kiss that the handsome prince awakens the enchanted princess. This kiss first appeared in Charles Perrault's version of 1697, 'La Belle au bois dormant'. But in fact, 'Sleeping Beauty' dates back to two earlier romances. 'Perceforest' and 'Pentamerone'. In those stories, the handsome prince finds the sleeping beauty, falls in love with her, rapes her and leaves.

4. The Kiss That Cost Thomas Saverland His Nose (1837)

In 1837, at the dawn of the Victorian era in Great Britain, Thomas Saverland attempted to kiss Caroline Newton in a lighthearted manner. Rejecting Saverland's pass, Miss Newton not so lightheartedly bit off part of his nose. Saverland took Newton to court, but she was acquitted. 'When a man kisses a woman against her will,' ruled the judge, 'she is fully entitled to bite his nose, if she so pleases.' 'And eat it up,' added a barrister.

5. *The Kiss* by François Auguste Rodin (1886)

One of the most renowned sculptures in the Western world is *The Kiss*, sculpted by French artist François Auguste Rodin in 1886. Inspired by Dante, the figure of two nude lovers kissing brought the era of classical art to an end. Rodin described *The Kiss* as 'complete in itself and artificially set apart from the surrounding world'.

6. The First Kiss Recorded on Film (1896)

The first kiss ever to be recorded in a film occurred in Thomas Edison's *The Kiss*, between John C. Rice and May Irwin in April 1896. Adapted from a short scene in the Broadway comedy *The Widow Jones*, *The Kiss* was filmed by Raff and Gammon for nickelodeon audiences. Its running time was less than 30 seconds.

7. The Most Often Kissed Statue in History (late-1800s)

The figure of Guidarello Guidarelli, a fearless sixteenth-century Italian soldier, was sculpted in marble by Tullio Lombardo (c. 1455–1532) and displayed at the Academy of Fine

Arts in Ravenna, Italy. During the late 1800s a rumour started that any woman who kissed the reclining, armour-clad statue would marry a wonderful gentleman. More than five million superstitious women have since kissed Guidarelli's cold marble lips. Consequently, the soldier's mouth has acquired a faint reddish glow.

8. The Movie With 191 Kisses (1926)

In 1926 Warner Brothers Studios starred John Barrymore in *Don Juan*. During the course of the film (2 hours, 47 minutes), the amorous adventurer bestows a total of 191 kisses on a number of beautiful señoritas – an average of one every 53 seconds.

9. The Longest Kiss on Film (1941)

The longest kiss in movie history is between Jane Wyman and Regis Toomey in the 1941 production of *You're in the Army Now*. The Lewis Seiler comedy about two vacuum-cleaner salesmen features a scene in which Toomey and Wyman hold a single kiss for 3 minutes and 5 seconds (or 4% of the film's running time).

10. The VJ-Day Kiss (1945)

When the news of Japan's surrender was announced in New York City's Times Square on August 14, 1945, *Life* photojournalist Alfred Eisenstaedt photographed a jubilant sailor clutching a nurse in a back-bending passionate kiss to vent his joy. The picture became an icon of the cathartic celebration that erupted over the end of the war. Over the years, at least three nurses and ten sailors claimed to be the people in the photo. Since Eisenstaedt had lost his notes and negatives by the time the claimants came forward, he was never able to say definitively who was in the photo.

11. The Kiss at L'Hôtel de Ville (1950)

A famous 1950 photograph of a young couple kissing on the streets of Paris – 'Le Baiser de l'Hôtel de Ville' – found itself under an international media spotlight when, four decades after the picture was taken, the photo became a commercial success, drawing out of the woodwork dozens of people who claimed to have been the photo's unidentified kissers. The black-and-white snapshot – originally taken for *Life* magazine by Robert Doisneau as part of his series on the Parisian working class – made Doisneau wealthy when, between 1986 and 1992, it became a bestseller through poster and postcard reprints. Among those who subsequently identified themselves as the kissers were Denise and Jean-Louis Lavergne, who sued Doisneau for $100,000 after he rejected their claim. They lost their case when it was determined, in 1993, that the kissers were actually two professional models (and real-life lovers), Françoise Bornet and Jacques Cartaud.

12. The First Interracial Kiss on US Television (1968)

NBC's *Star Trek* was the first programme to show a white man kissing a black woman. In the episode 'Plato's Children', aliens with psychic powers force Captain Kirk (William Shatner) to kiss Lt. Uhura (Nichelle Nichols).

13. The Majorca, Spain, Kiss-in (1969)

In 1969 an effort was made to crack down on young lovers who were smooching in public in the town of Inca on the island of Majorca. When the police chief began handing out citations that cost offenders 500 pesetas per kiss, a group of 30 couples protested by staging a kiss-in at the harbour at Cala Figuera. Following a massive roundup by police, the amorous rebels were fined 45,000 pesetas for their defiant canoodling and then released.

14. The Homosexual Kiss in *Sunday, Bloody Sunday* (1971)

One cinema kiss that turned heads among the movie-going public was between two male actors, Peter Finch and Murray Head, in the 1971 film *Sunday, Bloody Sunday*. The British tale of a bisexual love triangle included a medium close-up shot of this kiss in a scene originally planned to have featured only an embrace from afar. Director John Schlesinger commented that Finch and Head 'were certainly less shocked by the kiss than the technicians on the set were. When Finch was asked about the scene by somebody on TV, he said, "I did it for England."'

15. The Kiss of Humility (1975)

In an unprecedented gesture of humility, Pope Paul VI kissed the feet of Metropolitan Meliton of Chalcedon, envoy of Patriarch Demetrios I, who was head of the Eastern Orthodox Church, during a Mass at the Sistine Chapel in Rome in 1975. The two men were commemorating the tenth anniversary of the lifting of excommunications that the churches of Constantinople and Rome had conferred on each other during the eleventh century. Taken aback by the pontiff's dramatic action, Meliton attempted to kiss the pope's feet in return but the pope prevented him from doing so. Meliton instead kissed his hand.

16. The Kiss That Didn't Happen (1975)

King Faisal of Saudi Arabia was engaged in discussions with the Kuwait oil minister when the king's nephew, Prince Faisal ibn Mussad Abdel Aziz, burst into the office unannounced. The king stood and, assuming that the prince wished to offer him holy greetings for Mohammed's birthday, lowered his head and waited for the traditional kiss. It never arrived.

Instead the prince fired a bullet into the king's head, and another into his neck, killing him.

17. The Kiss That Cost $1,260 (1977)

Ruth van Herpen visited an art gallery in Oxford, England, in 1977 and kissed a painting by American artist Jo Baer, leaving red lipstick stains on the $18,000 work. Restoration costs were reported to be as much as $1,260. Appearing in court, van Herpen explained, 'I only kissed it to cheer it up. It looked so cold.'

18. The Kiss That Caused a Censorship Debate (1978)

The first kiss to reach the movie screen in India was between actor Shashi Kapoor and actress Zeenat Aman in the 1978 film *Love Sublime*. This landmark kiss, a product of new film guidelines, triggered a nationwide debate over censorship. Kapoor felt that the increased creative freedom would only add logic to Indian love stories and result in less cinema violence. Chief minister and film actor M.G. Ramachandran called for a mass protest, labelling the kissing scenes 'an insult'.

19. The First Lesbian Kiss on American Commercial Television (1991)

The first visible kiss between two women on an American network television series took place in 1991 on the show *L.A. Law*, when Michelle Greene kissed Amanda Donohoe. However, it was a later kiss, on the March 1, 1994, ABC-TV broadcast of the situation comedy *Roseanne* that caused a sensation. In a controversial scene well-publicised in the press, guest star Mariel Hemingway kisses series star Roseanne Arnold on the mouth. The kiss occurs in a 'gay bar' setting, and Hemingway portrays a lesbian stripper whose kiss causes Roseanne to question her own sensibilities. The episode (whose script originally included a second kiss between two additional women) became the subject of much high-profile bickering between ABC executives and series producers Tom and Roseanne Arnold during the weeks prior to its airing. Up to the eleventh hour, the very inclusion of the kiss appeared to remain in question, prompting protests by gay rights organisations. ABC finally let the kiss happen, but added a viewer warning at the start of the episode.

The first lesbian kiss on British TV was broadcast two years later, on Christmas Eve 1993, when *Brookside*'s Beth (Anna Friel) and Margaret (Nicola Stephenson), shared an eight-second smooch.

20. The Sexual Harassment Kiss (1996)

Six-year-old Johnathan Prevette, a first-grader at Southwest Elementary School in Lexington, North Carolina, kissed a classmate on the cheek. A teacher saw the September 19, 1996, incident and reported it to the school principal, Lisa Horne, who punished Johnathan by keeping him from attending an ice cream party and ordering him to spend a day in a disciplinary programme. But Johnathan's mother called a local radio talk show, word of the incident spread and within six months the US Department of Education had rewritten its sexual harassment guidelines to omit kisses by first-graders. For the record, Johnathan said that the girl asked him for a kiss.

21. The MTV Celebrity Kissfest (2003)

For the opening number of the 2003 MTV Video Music

Awards, Britney Spears and Christina Aguilera sang Madonna's 1984 hit 'Like a Virgin' while wearing white wedding gowns. As the music segued into Madonna's latest hit 'Hollywood', Madonna stepped out of a wedding cake wearing a tuxedo. What followed was a drag show of sorts with Madonna playing the groom and Britney and Christina the virginal brides. The performance climaxed with a French kiss between Madonna and Britney and then between Madonna and Christina. The kisses overshadowed the awards themselves and were front-page news around the world.

22. Big Brother in Bahrain (2004)

Bahrain-based MBC-TV attempted to introduce a Middle Eastern version of the voyeuristic reality show 'Big Brother' to Arabic-speaking audiences. A few minutes into the first episode, Abdel Hakim of Saudi Arabia kissed Kawthar of Tunisia. This ran so counter to cultural tradition that public protests broke out and the show was cancelled after only two weeks.

— D.B.

6 Positions for Sexual Intercourse – in Order of Popularity

Gershon Legman, an American who wrote about sex, calculated that there are more than 4 million possible ways for men and women to have sexual intercourse with each other. Most of these 'postures', as he called them, are probably variations on the six main positions that Alfred C. Kinsey used as categories in the questionnaires on sexual habits which were the basis for his *Kinsey Reports* in 1948 and 1953.

The *Kama Sutra*, a Hindu love manual written sometime between AD300 and 540, lists many imaginative and acrobatic variations on these positions – for example, the Bamboo Cleft, the Crab, the Wild Boar; some *Kama Sutra* experts suggest that people try out difficult positions in the water first. Chinese pillow books, written more than 400 years ago, show more feasible positions with titles like 'Two Dragons Exhausted by Battle' and name the parts of the body equally poetically – the penis is called the 'jade stem' and the clitoris, the 'pearl on the jade step'.

According to these sources, interpretations of ancient art, and anthropological studies, humans have changed their preference rankings of sexual positions – the 'missionary' (man-on-top) position, overwhelmingly the number-one choice of the Americans Kinsey studied, was not that high on the lists of ancient Greeks and Romans, primitive tribes, or many other groups.

The advantages and disadvantages of each position are taken from Albert Ellis's *The Art and Science of Love* and from *Human Sexual Inadequacy* by William H. Masters and Virginia E. Johnson.

1. Man on Top

To many people this is the only position considered biologically 'natural', though other primates use the rear-entry position almost exclusively. Called the 'missionary' position because it was introduced to native converts – who liked to make fun of it – by Christian missionaries who regarded other positions as sinful.

Advantage: Allows face-to-face intimacy, deep thrusting by male, pace setting by male.

Disadvantage: Does not allow good control for the premature ejaculator, or freedom of movement for the woman.

Chances for conception: Good.

2. Woman on Top

Shown in ancient art as most common position in Ur, Greece, Rome, Peru, India, China and Japan. Roman poet Martial portrayed Hector and Andromache in this position. Generally avoided by those at lower educational levels, according to Kinsey, because it seems to make the man less masculine, the woman less feminine.

Advantages: Allows freedom of movement for women, control for premature ejaculators, caressing of female by male. Most often results in orgasm for women. Good when the man is tired.

Disadvantage: Too acrobatic for some women.

Chances for conception: Not good.

3. Side By Side

From Ovid, a poet of ancient Rome: 'Of love's thousand ways, a simple way and with the least labour, this is: to lie on the right side, and half supine withal.'

Advantages: Allows manipulation of clitoris, freedom of movement for man and woman. Good for tired or convalescent people, and premature ejaculators, as well as pregnant women.

Disadvantage: Does not allow easy entry.

Chances for conception: Okay.

4. Rear Entrance

Frequently used by 15 per cent of married women. Favoured by primates and early Greeks. Rejected by many Americans because of its 'animal origins' and lack of face-to-face intimacy.

Advantages: Allows manual stimulation of clitoris. Exciting for men who are turned on by female buttocks. Good for pregnant women, males with small penises, women with large vaginas.

Disadvantages: Does not allow easy entry or face-to-face intimacy. Penis tends to fall out.

Chances for conception: Good.

5. Sitting

According to Kinsey, learned by many while 'making out' in back seats of cars.

Advantages: Allows clitoral contact with male body, free movement, intimacy. Good for male who wants to hold off orgasm, pregnant women.

Disadvantages: Does not allow vigorous thrusting. Sometimes tiring. Penetration may be too deep.

Chances for conception: Poor.

6. Standing

Has echoes of a 'quickie' against an alley wall with a prostitute, therefore exciting. Indian lotus position: each stands on one leg, wraps other around partner.

Advantages: Allows caressing. Exciting, can flow from dancing, taking shower.

Disadvantages: Does not allow much thrusting. Entry difficult, particularly when one partner is taller than the other. Tiring. Not good for pregnant women.

Chances for conception: Poor.

— A.E.

12 Foods Claimed to be Aphrodisiacs

1. Asparagus

Asparagus contains a diuretic that increases the amount of urine excreted and excites the urinary passages. The vegetable is rich in potassium, phosphorus and calcium – all necessary for maintenance of a high energy level. However, it also contains aspartic acid, which neutralises excess amounts of ammonia in one's body and may cause apathy and sexual uninterest.

2. Caviar

In addition to being nutritious (30% protein), caviar has been considered an aphrodisiac because of its obvious place in the reproductive process. All fish and their by-products have been linked to the myth of Aphrodite, the goddess of love who was born from the foam of the sea.

3. Eel

Eel, like most fish, is rich in phosphorus and has an excitant effect on the bladder. In addition to its general associations with the aphrodisiac effect of fish, it has probably been favoured as an aphrodisiac because of its phallic appearance.

4. Garlic

Both Eastern and Western cultures have long regarded garlic as an aphrodisiac. The Greeks and Romans sang its praises and oriental lovers claimed to be towers of strength because of eating it.

5. Ginseng

The Chinese call ginseng the 'elixir of life' and have used it for more than 5,000 years. Although medical opinion is sharply divided as to its merits, Russian experiments claim that ginseng increases sexual energy and has a general healing and rejuvenating influence on the body.

6. Green M&Ms

Mars, who make M&Ms, have consistently denied that green M&Ms have any effect on the libido. Nobody is sure how the rumour started, but in 1996 Mars ran an ad in which comedian Dennis Miller asks a female green M&M, 'Is it true what they say about the green ones?'

7. Honey

Honey is highly nutritious and rich in minerals, amino acids, enzymes and B-complex vitamins. Galen, Ovid and Sheikh Nefzawi, author of *The Perfumed Garden*, believed that honey has outstanding aphrodisiac powers.

8. Lobster

The lobster has been described as an amatory excitant by many writers, including Henry Fielding in *Tom Jones*. In addition, it shares the Aphrodite-derived power attributed to all seafood.

9. Oysters

Oysters are one of the most renowned aphrodisiac foods. Like other seafoods, they are rich in phosphorus. Although they are not a high source of energy, oysters are easily digestible. Among the eminent lovers who have vouched for oysters was Casanova, who called them 'a spur to the spirit and to love'.

10. Peaches

'Venus owns this tree . . . the fruit provokes lust . . .' wrote herbalist Nicholas Culpeper. The Chinese considered the fruit's sweet juices symbolic of the effluvia of the vagina, and both the Chinese and Arabs regard its deep fur-edged cleft as symbolic of the female genitalia. A 'peach house' was once a common English slang term for a brothel.

11. Tomatoes

When they were first brought from South America to Europe, tomatoes were thought to be the forbidden fruit of Eden. They were also celebrated as a sexual stimulant and nick-named 'love apples'.

12. Truffles

Truffles, the expensive underground fungi, are similar to oysters in that they are composed mostly of water and are rich in protein. Rabelais, Casanova, George Sand, Sade, Napoleon and Mme Pompadour are a few of the many notables who have praised the truffle's aphrodisiac powers. An ancient French proverb warns: 'Those who wish to lead virtuous lives should abstain from truffles.'

– R.H.

10 Men Who Cried In Public

1. Jesus Christ, Religious Leader

After Lazarus died, Jesus led his disciples to visit Lazarus's sisters, Mary and Martha. When the friends of Lazarus agreed to show Jesus the cave where Lazarus's body was laid, Jesus wept.

2. Bill Clinton, American President

On the morning of his inauguration, President Clinton and his family attended services at Washington's Metropolitan African Methodist Episcopal church. As the choir sang hymns, tears rolled down Clinton's cheeks. Clinton teared up frequently as his years in office continued. Once, when caught on camera laughing and joking at a funeral, Clinton suddenly realised he was being filmed. Having learned 'the Nixon lesson', he instantly grew serious and tears came to his eyes.

Right-wing TV host Rush Limbaugh played the tape in slow motion repeatedly, sending his studio audience into fits of mirth. Tom Lutz, the author of *Crying: The Natural & Cultural History of Tears*, observed that crying for male politicians was 'a 1990s version of kissing babies'.

3. David, Warrior King

When David and his troops returned to the city of Ziklag, after being sent home by the princes of the Philistines, they discovered that the Amalekites had invaded the city and taken captive all of the women and children, including David's two wives. David and his followers immediately 'lifted up their voices and wept until they had no more power to weep'.

4. Paul Gascoigne, English Footballer

Paul Gascoigne arrived at the Italia 90 World Cup as an up-and-coming young footballer with a gift for the unexpected on the field and a reputation for being, in his manager's words, 'as daft as a brush' off it. He left it a national folk hero. And all because millions of English football fans, glued to their TV sets back home, saw him weep. In the semi-final England were playing old rivals Germany – then still just West Germany. Gazza, whose performances in earlier rounds had helped his team to overcome a poor start to the competition, was again playing like a man inspired. Then tragedy struck. Gascoigne was booked for a reckless tackle. Even if England made it to the final, he would not play in the match. As the realisation hit home, Gazza's face crumpled and the tears began to flow. England went on to lose the match on penalties but Gazza had been taken to the nation's hearts and all the sorry antics of his later career have been unable quite to destroy that earlier image of him as a little boy lost on the world football stage.

5. John Lee Hooker, American Blues Musician

Hooker, the revered American blues musician, told an interviewer in 1998, 'You can't get no deeper than me and my guitar. I open my mouth, and it's there. I get so deep the teardrops come to my eyes. That's why I wear my dark glasses, so you won't see the teardrops.'

6. Michael Jordan, American Basketball Player

Michael Jordan cried openly when, while playing with the Chicago Bulls, he won his first NBA title in 1991 and this drew no comment from the press. Then, when he won his fourth title in 1996, he wept once more, falling onto the floor in a foetal position and sobbing when the game ended. This time TV announcers explained that Jordan's father had been murdered a year and a half before; the game was played on Father's Day, and Jordan had made an incredible comeback after retiring for two years.

7. Richard Nixon, American President

During a 1977 television interview, Nixon told David Frost, 'I never cry – except in public.' Nixon's most famous public weep occurred in 1952 after he made his notorious 'Checkers speech' and Dwight Eisenhower decided to allow him to remain on the Republican ticket as the vice-presidential candidate. Watching this performance, Nixon's college drama coach, Albert Upton, who had taught the future politician how to cry, remarked, 'Here goes my actor.'

8. Elvis Presley, American Singer

Presley cried so frequently in public that his nicknames included 'The Cry Guy', 'The Prince of Wails', 'The Golden Tearjerker', 'The Cheerful Tearful', 'Squirt-Gun Eyes' and 'America's Number One Public Weeper'.

9. Nikolai Ryzhkov, Russian Prime Minister

Ryzhkov was Prime Minister during Mikhail Gorbachev's reign. He received his nickname, 'The Weeping Bolshevik', for crying in front of the press when visiting Armenia after the brutal earthquake of 1988. Opposition critics treated him as an object of ridicule, a pathetic clown. Running for Parliament in 1995, he countered accusations that tears proved him too weak to hold a position of power, implying others would have wept had they seen the same horrors. By changing public opinion to that of viewing tears not as a weakness but as a sign of humanity, Ryzhkov won the election.

10. Norman Schwarzkopf, American Military Leader

Towards the end of the 1991 Persian Gulf War, General Schwarzkopf was interviewed on television by Barbara Walters. His eyes welled up with tears as he answered personal questions. Walters said, 'Generals don't cry'. Schwarzkopf replied, 'Grant, after Shiloh, went back and cried. Sherman went back and cried ... and these are tough old guys ... Lincoln cried.' He added that he held back his tears in front of his troops during the war for the purpose of morale; although he could cry in front of them during a Christmas Eve service, where he was embodying the role of father figure, rather than commanding officer.

18 Stupid Thieves and 3 Dishonourable Mentions

I. Showing Off His Booty

Charles Taylor of Wichita, Kansas, was arrested for robbing a shoe store at knifepoint and stealing a $69-pair of size 10 ½ tan hiking boots on December 18, 1996. At his trial three months later, Taylor arrogantly rested his feet on the defence table. He was wearing a pair of size 10 ½ tan hiking boots. The judge, James Fleetwood was incredulous. 'I leaned over and stared,' he later said. 'Surely nobody would be so stupid as to wear the boots he stole to his trial.' But it turned out that one person was that stupid. Taylor was convicted of aggravated robbery and sent back to jail in his stocking feet.

2. Wrong Place, Wrong Time

On November 29, 1978, David Goodhall and two female accomplices entered a home supplies shop in Barnsley, South Yorkshire, intending to engage in a bit of shoplifting. After stuffing a pair of curtains into a plastic carrier bag, the threesome attempted to leave by separate exits. However, they were apprehended immediately by several store detectives. Goodhall and his cohorts had failed to notice that the shop, at that very moment, was hosting a convention of store detectives.

3. Checking Out

Eighteen-year-old Charles A. Meriweather broke into a home in Northwest Baltimore on the night of November 22–23, 1978, raped the woman who lived there, and then ransacked the house. When he discovered she had only $11.50 in cash, he asked her 'How do you pay your bills?'

She replied, 'By cheque' and he ordered her to write out a cheque for $30. Then he changed his mind and upped it to $50.

'Who shall I make it out to?' asked the woman, a 34-year-old government employee.

'Charles A. Meriweather,' said Charles A. Meriweather, adding, 'It better not bounce or I'll be back.'

Meriweather was arrested several hours later.

4. Just Reward

Every night, Mrs Hollis Sharpe of Los Angeles took her miniature poodle, Jonathan, out for a walk so that he could do his duty. A responsible and considerate citizen, Mrs Sharpe always brought along with her a newspaper and a plastic bag to clean up after him, 'You have to think of your neighbours,' she explained. On the night of November 13, 1974, Jonathan had finished his business and Mrs Sharpe was walking home with the bag in her right hand when a mugger attacked her from behind, shoved her to the ground, grabbed her plastic bag, jumped into a car, and drove off with the spoils of his crime. Mrs Sharpe suffered a broken arm, but remained good-humoured about the incident. 'I only wish there had been a little more in the bag,' she said.

5. A Minor Detail

Edward McAlea put on a stocking mask, burst into a jewellery store in Liverpool, and pointed a revolver at the three men inside. 'This is a stick up,' he said. 'Get down.' None of them did, since all of them noticed the red plastic stopper in the muzzle of McAlea's toy gun. After a brief scuffle, McAlea escaped, but not before he had pulled off his mask. The jeweller recognised him as a customer from the day before, and McAlea was apprehended.

6. Keep the Change

In 1977, a thief in Southampton, England, came up with a clever method of robbing the cash register at a local supermarket. After collecting a basket full of groceries, he approached the checkout area and placed a £10 note on the counter. The grocery clerk took the bill and opened the cash register, at which point the thief snatched the contents and ran off. It turned out to be a bad deal for the thief, since the till contained only £4.37 and the thief ended up losing £5.63.

7. The Weld-planned Robbery

On the night of August 23–24, 1980, a well-organised gang of thieves began their raid on the safe of the leisure-centre office in Chichester, Sussex, by stealing a speedboat. Using water skis to paddle across the lake, they picked up their equipment and paddled on to the office. However, what they thought were cutting tools turned out to be welding gear, and they soon managed to seal the safe completely shut. The next morning it took the office staff an hour to hammer and chisel the safe open again.

8. Stuck for Life

There is a whole sub-genre of stupid thieves who get stuck while trying to sneak into buildings through chimneys and air vents that turn out to be narrower at the bottom than at the top. However, none has quite met the fate that befell Calvin Wilson of Natchez, Mississippi. A burglar with a criminal record, Wilson disappeared in 1985. The following year, a body found on the banks of the Mississippi River was identified – incorrectly, as it turned out – as that of Wilson.

Fifteen years later, in January 2001, masons renovating a historic building in Natchez discovered a fully-clothed skeleton in the chimney. Lying next to the skeleton was a wallet belonging to Calvin Wilson. Adams County sheriffs theorised that Wilson had tried to enter the building, which was then a gift shop, through the chimney, fallen in head first and become stuck in the chimney, unable to call for help.

9. Who Was That Masked Man?

Clive Bunyan ran into a store in Cayton, near Scarborough, England, and forced the shop assistant to give him £157 from the till. Then he made his getaway on his motorbike. To hide his identity, Bunyan had worn his full-face helmet as a mask. It was a smooth successful heist, except for one detail. He had forgotten that across his helmet, in inch-high letters, were the words, 'Clive Bunyan – Driver'. Bunyan was arrested and ordered to pay for his crime by doing 200 hours of community service.

10. Burglary by the Number

Terry Johnson had no trouble identifying the two men who burgled her Chicago apartment at 2.30 a.m. on August 17, 1981. All she had to do was write down the number on the police badge that one of them was wearing and the identity number on the fender of their squad car. The two officers – Stephen Webster, 33, and Tyrone Pickens, 32 – had actually committed the crime in full uniform, while on duty, using police department tools.

11. The Worst Lawyer

Twenty-five-year-old Marshall George Cummings, Jr., of Tulsa, Oklahoma, was charged with attempted robbery in connection with a bag-snatching at a shopping centre on October 14, 1976. During the trial the following January, Cummings chose to act as his own attorney. While cross-examining the victim, Cummings asked, 'Did you get a good look at my face when I took your bag?' Cummings later de-cided to turn over his defence to a public defender, but it was too late. He was convicted and sentenced to 10 years in prison.

12. Safe at Last

On the night of June 12, 1991, John Meacham, Joseph Plante and Joe Laattsch were burgling a soon-to-be demolished bank building in West Covina, California, when Meacham came upon an empty vault. He called over his accomplices and invited them inside to check out the acoustics. Then he closed the vault door so they could appreciate the full effect. Unfortunately, the door locked. Meacham spent 40 minutes trying to open it, without success. Finally he called the fire department, who called the police. After seven hours, a concrete-sawing firm was able to free the locked-up robbers, after which they were transported to another building they could not get out of.

13. Big Mouth

Dennis Newton was on trial in 1985 for armed robbery in Oklahoma City. Assistant District Attorney Larry Jones asked one of the witnesses, the supervisor of the store that had been robbed, to identify the robber. When she pointed to the defendant, Newton jumped to his feet, accused the witness of lying, and said, 'I should have blown your –ing head off!' After a moment of stunned silence, he added, 'If I'd been the one that was there.' The jury sentenced Jones to 30 years in prison.

14. Inconvenience Store

In December 1989, three 15-year-old boys stole a car in Prairie Village, Kansas, and stopped off at the nearest convenience store to ask directions back to Missouri. Except that it wasn't a convenience store – it was a police station. At the same moment, a description of the stolen vehicle was broadcast over the police station public address system. The car thieves tried to escape, but were quickly apprehended.

15. Wrong Fence

Stephen Le and two juvenile companions tried to break into a parked pickup truck in Larkspur, California, on the night of September 27, 1989. But the owner caught them in the act, chased them, and hailed a police car. Le and one of his friends climbed a fence and ran. It soon became apparent that they had chosen the wrong fence – this one surrounded the property of San Quentin prison. The suspects were booked for investigation of auto burglary and trespassing on state property, although charges were never filed. 'Nothing like this has ever happened here before,' said Lieutenant Cal White. 'People just don't break into prison every day.'

16. Birdbrained Thieves

During a midnight raid in May 1997, thieves climbed a 6-ft fence at the home of Bob Hodgson in Ryton, near Gateshead, Tyne and Wear. They broke open two locks and stole 40 homing pigeons worth £1,000. It was a clever, well-organised robbery – except for one minor problem: homing pigeons fly home. That is exactly what all but the eight youngest pigeons did.

17. Returning to the Scene of the Crime

While training to become a military police officer, US Army Private Daniel Bowden was taught how criminals commit bank robberies. As it turned out, Bowden was not a very good student. In May 1997, he robbed a federal credit union in Fort Belvoir, Virginia, making away with $4,759 in cash. The following week, Bowden, who had not worn a mask during the commission of his crime, returned to the same bank and tried to deposit the money into his own personal account. He was immediately recognised by a teller, who alerted the military police.

18. Shooting Himself in the Foot

In February 2004, Carlos Henrique Auad of Petropolis, Brazil, broke into a bar near his home and stole a television set. A few nights later, Auad tried to break into the same bar through the roof. This time, carrying a gun, he slipped and fell and shot himself in the right foot. Auad went straight home, but failed to notice that he left a trail of blood that led right to his door. He was arrested by police, who found the television set.

DISHONOURABLE MENTIONS

1. Stupid Drug Dealer

Alfred Acree Jr was sitting in a van in Charles City, Virginia, on April 7, 1993, with three friends and at least 30 small bags of cocaine. When sheriff's deputies surrounded the van, Acree raced into a dark, wooded area by the side of the road. He weaved in and out of the trees in an attempt to evade his pursuers. He thought he had done a pretty good job – and was amazed when the deputies caught him (and found $800 worth of cocaine in his pockets). What Acree had forgotten was that he was wearing LA Tech sneakers that sent out a red light every time they struck the ground. While Acree was tiring himself zigzagging through the forest, the sheriffs were calmly following the blinking red lights.

2. Stupid Drug Traffickers

Drug traffickers Edward Velez and José Gonzales were transporting 2 lb of methamphetamine by aeroplane on the night of December 7, 1994. They had planned to land at a small airport in Turlock, California, but Velez, the pilot, miscalculated and touched down at a different airport 20 miles away. Unfortunately for Velez and Gonzalez, the airport was part of the Castle Air Force Base, where air force pilots were practicing night touch-and-go landings. Security police intercepted the plane as soon as it landed.

3. Stupid Terrorist

In early 1994 an Islamic fundamentalist group in Jordan launched a terrorist campaign that included attacks against secular sites such as video stores and supermarkets that sold liquor. During the late morning of February 1, Eid Saleh al Jahaleen, a 31-year-old plumber, entered the Salwa Cinema in the city of Zarqa. The cinema was showing soft-core pornographic films from Turkey. Jahaleen, who was apparently paid $50 to plant a bomb, had never seen soft-core porn and became entranced. When the bomb went off, he was still in his seat. Jahaleen lost both legs in the explosion.

10 Largest Arms Exporters (1998–2002)

		$ Millions (US)
1.	USA	37,723
2.	Russia	20,741
3.	France	8,312
4.	Germany	4,954
5.	UK	4,811
6.	Ukraine	2,673
7.	Italy	1,787
8.	China	1,561
9.	Netherlands	1,520
10.	Belarus	1,142

Source: Stockholm International Peace Research Institute (*SIPRI Yearbook 2002*)

18 Secret Armies of the CIA

1. Ukrainian Partisans

From 1945 to 1952 the CIA trained and aerially supplied Ukrainian partisan units which had originally been organised by the Germans to fight the Soviets during WWII. For seven years, the partisans, operating in the Carpathian Mountains, made sporadic attacks. Finally, in 1952, a massive Soviet military force wiped them out.

2. Chinese Brigade in Burma

After the Communist victory in China, Nationalist Chinese soldiers fled into northern Burma. During the early 1950s, the CIA used these soldiers to create a 12,000-man brigade which made raids into Red China. However, the Nationalist soldiers found it more profitable to monopolise the local opium trade.

3. Guatemalan Rebel Army

After Guatemalan president Jacobo Arbenz legalised that country's Communist party and expropriated 400,000 acres of United Fruit banana plantations, the CIA decided to overthrow his government. Guatemalan rebels were trained in Honduras and backed up with a CIA air contingent of bombers and fighter planes. This army invaded Guatemala in 1954, promptly toppling Arbenz's regime.

4. Sumatran Rebels

In an attempt to overthrow Indonesian president Sukarno in 1958, the CIA sent paramilitary experts and radio operators to the island of Sumatra to organise a revolt. With CIA air support, the rebel army attacked but was quickly defeated. The American government denied involvement even after a CIA B-26 was shot down and its CIA pilot, Allen Pope, was captured.

5. Khamba Horsemen

After the 1950 Chinese invasion of Tibet, the CIA began recruiting Khamba horsemen – fierce warriors who supported

Tibet's religious leader, the Dalai Lama – as they escaped into India in 1959. These Khambas were trained in modern warfare at Camp Hale, high in the Rocky Mountains near Leadville, Colorado. Transported back to Tibet by the CIA-operated Air America, the Khambas organised an army numbering at its peak some 14,000. By the mid-1960s the Khambas had been abandoned by the CIA but they fought on alone until 1970.

6. Bay of Pigs Invasion Force

In 1960 CIA operatives recruited 1,500 Cuban refugees living in Miami and staged a surprise attack on Fidel Castro's Cuba. Trained at a base in Guatemala, this small army – complete with an air force consisting of B-26 bombers – landed at the Bay of Pigs on April 17, 1961. The ill-conceived, poorly planned operation ended in disaster, since all but 150 men of the force were either killed or captured within three days.

7. L'Armée Clandestine

In 1962 CIA agents recruited Meo tribesmen living in the mountains of Laos to fight as guerrillas against Communist Pathet Lao forces. Called l'Armée Clandestine, this unit – paid, trained and supplied by the CIA – grew into a 30,000-man force. By 1975 the Meos – who had numbered a quarter of a million in 1962 – had been reduced to 10,000 refugees fleeing into Thailand.

8. Nung Mercenaries

A Chinese hill people living in Vietnam, the Nungs were hired and organised by the CIA as a mercenary force, during the Vietnam War. Fearsome and brutal fighters, the Nungs were employed throughout Vietnam and along the Ho Chi Minh Trail. The Nungs proved costly since they refused to fight unless constantly supplied with beer and prostitutes.

9. Peruvian Regiment

Unable to quell guerrilla forces in its eastern Amazonian provinces, Peru called on the US for help in the mid-1960s.

The CIA responded by establishing a fortified camp in the area and hiring local Peruvians who were trained by Green Beret personnel on loan from the US Army. After crushing the guerillas, the elite unit was disbanded because of fears it might stage a coup against the government.

10. Congo Mercenary Force

In 1964, during the Congolese Civil War, the CIA established an army in the Congo to back pro-Western leaders Cyril Adoula and Joseph Mobutu. The CIA imported European mercenaries and Cuban pilots – exiles from Cuba – to pilot the CIA air force, composed of transports and B-26 bombers.

11. The Cambodian Coup

For over 15 years the CIA had tried various unsuccessful means of deposing Cambodia's left-leaning Prince Norodom Sihanouk, including assassination attempts. However, in March 1970 a CIA-backed coup finally did the job. Funded by US tax dollars, armed with US weapons and trained by American Green Berets, anti-Sihanouk forces called Kampuchea

Khmer Krom (KKK) overran the capital of Phnom Penh and took control of the government. With the blessing of the CIA and the Nixon administration, control of Cambodia was placed in the hands of Lon Nol, who would later distinguish himself by dispatching soldiers to butcher tens of thousands of civilians.

12. Kurd Rebels

During the early 1970s the CIA moved into eastern Iraq to organise and supply the Kurds of that area, who were rebelling against the pro-Soviet Iraqi government. The real purpose behind this action was to help the Shah of Iran settle a border dispute with Iraq favourably. After an Iran–Iraq settlement was reached, the CIA withdrew its support from the Kurds, who were then crushed by the Iraqi Army.

13. Angola Mercenary Force

In 1975, after years of bloody fighting and civil unrest in Angola, Portugal resolved to relinquish its hold on the last of its African colonies. The transition was to take place on

November 11, with control of the country going to whichever political faction controlled the capital city of Luanda on that date. In the months preceding the change, three groups vied for power: the Popular Movement for the Liberation of Angola (MPLA), the National Front for the Liberation of Angola (FNLA) and the National Union for the Total Independence of Angola (UNITA). By July 1975 the Marxist MPLA had ousted the moderate FNLA and UNITA from Luanda, so the CIA decided to intervene covertly. Over $30 million was spent on the Angolan operation, the bulk of the money going to buy arms and pay French and South African mercenaries, who aided the FNLA and UNITA in their fight. Despite overwhelming evidence to the contrary, US officials categorically denied any involvement in the Angolan conflict. In the end, it was a fruitless military adventure, for the MPLA assumed power and controls Angola to this day.

14. Afghan Mujahedin

Covert support for the groups fighting against the Soviet invasion of Afghanistan began under President Jimmy

Carter in 1979, and was stepped up during the administration of Ronald Reagan. The operation succeeded in its initial goal, as the Soviets were forced to begin withdrawing their forces in 1987. Unfortunately, once the Soviets left, the US essentially ignored Afghanistan as it collapsed into a five-year civil war followed by the rise of the ultra-fundamentalist Taliban. The Taliban provided a haven for Osama bin Laden and al-Qaeda, the perpetrators of the 9/11 terrorist attacks in 2001.

15. Salvadoran Death Squads

As far back as 1964 the CIA helped form ORDEN and ANSESAL, two paramilitary intelligence networks that developed into the Salvadoran death squads. The CIA trained ORDEN leaders in the use of automatic weapons and surveillance techniques, and placed several leaders on the CIA payroll. The CIA also provided detailed intelligence on Salvadoran individuals later murdered by the death squads. During the civil war in El Salvador from 1980 to 1992, the death squads were responsible for 40,000 killings. Even after a public outcry forced President Reagan to denounce the death squads in 1984, CIA support continued.

16. Nicaraguan Contras

On November 23, 1981, President Ronald Reagan signed a top secret National Security Directive authorising the CIA to spend $19 million to recruit and support the Contras, opponents of Nicaragua's Sandinista government. In supporting the Contras, the CIA carried out several acts of sabotage without the Congressional intelligence committees giving consent – or even being informed beforehand. In response, Congress passed the Boland Amendment, prohibiting the CIA from providing aid to the Contras. Attempts to find alternate sources of funds led to the Iran-Contra scandal. It may also have led the CIA and the Contras to become actively involved in drug smuggling. In 1988 the Senate Subcommittee on Narcotics, Terrorism, and International Operations concluded that individuals in the Contra movement engaged in drug trafficking; that known drug traffickers provided assistance to the Contras; and that 'there are some serious questions as to whether or not US officials involved in Central America failed to address the drug issue for fear of jeopardising the war effort against Nicaragua'.

17. Haitian Coups

In 1988 the CIA attempted to intervene in Haiti's elections with a 'covert action program' to undermine the campaign of the eventual winner, Jean-Bertrand Aristide. Three years later, Aristide was overthrown in a bloody coup that killed more than 4,000 civilians. Many of the leaders of the coup had been on the CIA payroll since the mid-1980s. For example, Emmanuel 'Toto' Constant, the head of FRAPH, a brutal gang of thugs known for murder, torture and beatings, admitted to being a paid agent of the CIA. Similarly, the CIA-created Haitian National Intelligence Service (NIS), supposedly created to combat drugs, functioned during the coup as a 'political intimidation and assassination squad'. In 1994 an American force of 20,000 was sent to Haiti to allow Aristide to return. Ironically, even after this, the CIA continued working with FRAPH and the NIS. In 2004 Aristide was overthrown once again, with Aristide claiming that US forces had kidnapped him.

18. Venezuelan Coup Attempt

On April 11, 2002 Venezuelan military leaders attempted to overthrow the country's democratically-elected left-wing president, Hugo Chavez. The coup collapsed after two days, as hundreds of thousands of people took to the streets and as units of the military joined with the protestors. The administration of George W. Bush was the only democracy in the western hemisphere not to condemn the coup attempt. According to intelligence analyst Wayne Madsen, the CIA had actively organised the coup: 'The CIA provided Special Operations Group personnel, headed by a lieutenant colonel on loan from the US Special Operations Command at Fort Bragg, North Carolina, to help organise the coup against Chavez.'

– R.J.F. & C.F.

22 Cases of Animals and Insects Brought Before the Law

There has been a long and shocking tradition of punishing, excommunicating and killing animals for real or supposed crimes. In medieval times, animals were even put on the rack to extort confessions of guilt. Cases have been recorded and documented involving such unlikely creatures as flies, locusts, snakes, mosquitoes, caterpillars, eels, snails, beetles, grasshoppers, dolphins and most larger mammals. In seventeenth-century Russia, a goat was banished to Siberia. The belief that animals are morally culpable is happily out of fashion – but not completely, for even now, these travesties and comedies occasionally occur.

1. Canine Convict No. C2559

Rarely in American history has an animal served a prison term. Incredibly, it happened as recently as 1924, in Pike County, Pennsylvania. Pep, a male Labrador retriever, belonged to neighbours of Governor and Mrs Gifford Pinchot. A friendly dog, Pep unaccountably went wild one hot summer day and killed Mrs Pinchot's cat. An enraged Governor Pinchot presided over an immediate hearing and then a trial. Poor Pep had no legal counsel, and the evidence against him was damning. Pinchot sentenced him to life imprisonment. The no doubt bewildered beast was taken to the state penitentiary in Philadelphia. The warden, also bewildered, wondered whether he should assign the mutt an ID number like the rest of the cons. Tradition won out, and

Pep became No. c2559. The story has a happy ending: Pep's fellow inmates lavished him with affection, and he was allowed to switch cellmates at will. The prisoners were building a new penitentiary in Graterford, Pennsylvania, and every morning the enthusiastic dog boarded the bus for work upon hearing his number called. When the prison was completed, Pep was one of the first to move in. In 1930, after six years in prison (42 dog years), Pep died of old age.

2. The Rising Cost of Air Travel

In Tripoli in 1963, 75 carrier pigeons received the death sentence. A gang of smugglers had trained the birds to carry bank notes from Italy, Greece and Egypt into Libya. The court ordered the pigeons to be killed because 'They were too well trained and dangerous to be let loose.' The humans were merely fined.

3. Too Much Monkey Business

In 1905 the law against public cigarette smoking was violated in South Bend, Indiana. A showman's chimpanzee puffed tobacco in front of a crowd and was hauled before the court, where he was convicted and fined.

4. It's a Dog's Life

In 1933 four dogs in McGraw, New York, were prosecuted to the full extent of the law for biting six-year-old Joyce Hammond. In a full hearing before an audience of 150, their lawyer failed to save them from execution by the county veterinarian. Proclaimed justice A.P. McGraw: 'I know the value of a good dog. But this is a serious case . . . The dogs are criminals of the worst kind.'

5. A Hoof for a Hoof

The Wild West custom of killing a horse responsible for the death of a human was re-enacted by a group of Chicago gangsters in 1924. When the infamous Nails Morton died in Lincoln Park after being thrown from a riding horse, his buddies in Dion O'Banion's gang sought revenge. They kidnapped the animal from its stable at gunpoint and took it to the scene of the crime, where they solemnly executed it.

6. You Really Got a Hold On Me

In 1451 in Lausanne, a number of leeches were brought into an ecclesiastical court. We can only imagine their distress as they listened to the reading of a document demanding that they leave town. When the tenacious leeches stuck to their guns they were exorcised by the bishop-court.

7. Dogged by the Law

'Perverts transformed their stables into harems', wrote a French author in his legal history of the province of Lorraine. For centuries, bestiality was a regularly prosecuted crime, and as recently as 1940 a man was burned at the stake in Pont-à-Mousson, France, with three cows. The case of Guillaume Guyart in 1606 contains a surreal twist. Guyart was sentenced to be hanged and burned for sodomy; his accomplice, a female dog, was to be knocked on the head and burned along with him. When Guyart managed to escape, the court decreed that his property be confiscated to pay for the costs of the trial. If the criminal were not caught, the judges ruled, the sentence would be carried out – a painting of Guyart would be hung from the scaffold. There is no record of the ultimate fate of the man or the dog.

8. The Barnyard Bordello

Puritan clergyman Cotton Mather left a rare account of an American buggery case. He wrote, 'on June 6, 1662, at New Haven, there was a most unparallelled wretch, one Potter by name, about 60 years of age, executed for damnable Beastialities [sic]'. Potter, it seems, began sodomising animals at the age of 10 and never stopped. At the same time, he was a devout churchgoer noted for his piety and for being 'zealous in reforming the sins of other people'. The man's wife, Mather wrote, 'had seen him confounding himself with a bitch ten years before; and he had excused himself as well as he could, but conjured her to keep it secret'. Potter then hanged the animal, presumably as an apology to his wife. Eventually, the law caught up with him, and he went to the gallows preceded by a cow, two heifers, three sheep and two sows. Watching his concubines die one by one, Potter was in tears by the time he approached the scaffold.

9. I'm Not That Kind of Girl

In Vanvres, France, in 1750, Jacques Ferron was caught in the act of love with a she-ass and sentenced to hang. Normally, his partner would have died as well – but members of the community took an unprecedented step. They signed a petition that they had known the she-ass for four years, that she had always been well behaved at home and abroad and had never caused a scandal of any kind. She was, they concluded, 'in all her habits of life a most honest creature'. As the result of this intervention, Ferron was hanged for sodomy, and the she-ass was acquitted.

10. Juvenile Delinquents?

The vast majority of prosecuted animals were pigs. In the Middle Ages they were frequently left unwatched, and they often harmed small children. Once arrested, they were usually placed in solitary confinement in the same jail with human criminals, registered as 'so-and-so's pig', and publicly hanged with all the formality of a typical medieval execution. In the annals of animal crime, there are many famous pig cases. One of the most fully documented and most unusual occurred in Savigny, France, in 1457. A sow and her six piglets were accused of 'wilfully and feloniously' murdering a five-year-old boy, Jean Martin. Found guilty, the sow was eventually hanged by its hind legs from the gallows. But the matter was not so simple: were the six piglets – who had been found stained with blood at the scene of the crime – also guilty? Their owner, Jean Bailly, was asked to post bail for them until a second trial and to take the accused back into his custody. Bailly said he didn't have the money, and furthermore, refused to make any promises about the piglets' future good behaviour. Three weeks later 'the six little porklets' went to court. Because of their youth and the lack of firm evidence of their guilt, the court was lenient. The piglets were given to a local noblewoman; Bailly did not have to pay, and the porklets could hold their heads high.

11. An Important Ruling

A significant pig case occurred in 1846 in Pleternica, Slavonia – it was one of the first times an animal's owner bore responsibility for damages. A pig ate the ears of a one-year-old girl and was given the usual death sentence. Its owner was sentenced to labour in order to provide a dowry for the earless girl, so that, despite her loss, she might someday find a husband.

12. Monkeying Around

As recently as January 23, 1962, an animal was called into the courtroom. Makao, a young cercopithecoid monkey, escaped from his master's apartment in Paris and wandered into an empty studio nearby. He bit into a tube of lipstick, destroyed some expensive knick-knacks and 'stole' a box that was later recovered – empty. The victims of Makao's pranks filed a complaint stating that the box had contained a valuable ring. The monkey's owner contended before the judge that his pet could not possibly have opened such a box. Makao was ordered to appear in court, where he deftly opened a series of boxes. His defence ruined, Makao's master was held liable for full damages.

13. A Happy Tail

In 1877 in New York City, Mary Shea, a woman of Celtic origin, was bitten on the finger by Jimmy, an organ-grinder's monkey. Mary demanded retribution, but the judge said he could not commit an animal. Miffed, Mary stormed out of the courtroom, snarling, 'This is a nice country for justice!' The monkey, who was dressed in a scarlet coat and velvet cap, showed his appreciation: he curled his tail around the gas fixture on the judge's desk and tried to shake hands with him. The police blotter gave this record of the event: 'Name: Jimmy Dillio. Occupation: Monkey. Disposition: Discharged'.

14. Hard-boiled Criminal

One of the most celebrated animal trials was that of the rooster in Basel, Switzerland, which was accused in 1474 of laying an egg (without a yolk no less). It was a widely held belief that such eggs could be hatched by witches in league with Satan, giving birth to deadly winged snakes. The accused cock was in a tight spot, and even his defence attorney did not argue that the charges were false. He did argue that his client had no pact with the devil and that laying an egg was an unpremeditated and involuntary act. The judges were not impressed, and after a lengthy trial it was decided that the rooster was possessed by

Satan. The bird and the egg were burned at the stake before a huge crowd. The subject was being debated more than 200 years later, in 1710, when a Frenchman presented a paper before the Academy of Sciences stating that yolkless eggs were merely the occasional products of an ailing hen.

15. Women and Children First

In Stelvio, Italy, in 1519, field mice (referred to in a German account as *Lutmäusse* – they may have been moles) were accused of damaging crops by burrowing. They were granted a defence attorney, Hans Grienebner, so that they could 'show cause for their conduct by pleading their exigencies and distress'. He claimed that his clients were helpful citizens who ate harmful insects and enriched the soil. The prosecutor, Schwartz Mining, argued that the damage they caused was preventing local tenants from paying their rents. The judge was merciful. Though he exiled the animals, he assured them of safe conduct 'and an additional respite of 14 days to all those which are with young, and to such as are yet in their infancy'.

16. Putting the Bite on the Landlord

In the 1700s, an order of Franciscan friars in Brazil was driven to despair by the termites which were devouring not only the food and furniture, but also the very walls of the monastery. The monks pleaded with the bishop for an act of excommunication, and an ecclesiastical trial was held. When the accused defiantly failed to appear in court, they were appointed a lawyer. He made the usual speech about how all God's creatures deserved to eat, and he praised his clients' industry, which he said was far greater than that of the friars. Further, he argued that the termites had occupied the land long before the monks. The lengthy trial overflowed with complicated legal speeches and much passionate quoting of authorities. In the end, it was decided that the monks should give the termites their own plot of land. The judge's order was read aloud to the termite hills. According to a monk's document dated January, 1713, the termites promptly came out of the hills and marched in columns to their new home. Woodn't you know it?

17. A Cat-astrophic Ruling

It was an ancient Breton belief that tomcats had to be killed before reaching the age of seven, or they would kill their masters. One morning a farmer of Pleyben was found dead in his bed, his throat slit. The local judge had already arrested two servants, when the herdsman noticed the household cat in front of the hearth. Proclaiming, 'I for one know who the culprit is!' the herdsman pulled the following stunt: he tied a string to the dead man's wrist, ran the other end through a window, and gave it a tug from outside – thus 'shaking' the corpse's arm. Right in front of the judge, the tomcat calmly approached his 'revived' master in order to finish him off properly. The guilty cat was burned alive.

18. What's a Mayor To Do?

In Ansbach, Germany, in 1685, it was reported that a vicious wolf was ravaging herds and devouring women and children. The beast was believed to be none other than the town's deceased mayor, who had turned into a werewolf. A typical politician, the wolf/mayor was hard to pin down, but was finally captured and killed. The animal's carcass was then dressed in a flesh-coloured suit, a brown wig, and a long grey-white beard. Its snout was cut off and replaced with a mask of the mayor. By court order, the creature was hanged from a windmill. The weremayor's pelt was then stuffed and displayed in a town official's cabinet, to serve forever as proof of the existence of werewolves.

19. The Cruel Death of '5-ton Mary'

There are ancient records of the hangings of bulls and oxen, but there is only one known case of the hanging of an elephant – it happened in Erwin, Tennessee, on September 13, 1916. The Sparks Circus was stationed in Kingsport, Tennessee, when Mary, a veteran circus elephant, was being ridden to water by an inexperienced trainer, Walter Eldridge. On the way, Mary spotted a watermelon rind and headed for this snack. When Eldridge jerked hard on her head with a spear-tipped stick, Mary let out a loud trumpet, reached behind her with her trunk, and yanked the trainer off her back. Mary dashed Eldridge against a soft-drink stand and then walked over and stepped on his head. A Kingsport resident came running and fired five pistol shots into the huge animal. Mary groaned and shook but did not die – in fact, she performed in that night's show. The next day the circus moved to Erwin, where 'authorities' (no one is sure who) decreed that Mary should die on the gallows, to the great sorrow of her friends in the circus. She was taken to the Clinchfield railroad yards, where a large crowd was gathered. A $7/8$-in. chain was slung around her neck, and a 100-ton derrick hoisted her 5 ft in the air. The chain broke. The next chain held, and Mary died quickly. Her 5-ton corpse was buried with a steam shovel.

20. Free Speech

Carl Miles exhibited Blackie, his 'talking' cat, on street corners in Augusta, Georgia, and collected 'contributions'. Blackie could say two phrases: 'I love you' and 'I want my momma'. In 1981, the city of Augusta said the enterprise required a business licence and a fee, which Miles refused to pay. He sued the city council, arguing that the fee impinged on the cat's right to free speech. The judge actually heard

Blackie say 'I love you' in court. However, he ruled that the case was not a free speech issue. Since Blackie was charging money for his speech, the city was entitled to their fee. Miles paid $50 for the licence and Blackie went back to work. He died in 1992 at the age of 18.

21. Last-minute Escape

On September 30, 1982, Tucker, a 140-lb bull mastiff, ran into a neighbour's yard and attacked the neighbour's black miniature poodle, Bonnie. Tucker's owner, Eric Leonard, freed the poodle from Tucker's mouth, but the poodle had received critical injuries and died. A district court in Augusta, Maine, ruled that Tucker was a danger to other dogs and should be killed by intravenous injection. Leonard appealed to the Maine Supreme Court, but it upheld the lower court's ruling. In 1984, two days before his scheduled execution, the 'National Doggie Liberation Front' removed Tucker from the shelter where he was being held. What happened to Tucker is unknown.

22. Death-row Dog

The long arm of the law almost took the life of a 110-lb Akita named Taro, who got into trouble on Christmas Day of 1990. Owned by Lonnie and Sandy Lehrer of Haworth, New Jersey, Taro injured the Lehrers' 10-year-old niece, but how the injury occurred was in dispute. Police and doctors who inspected the injury said the dog bit the girl's lower lip. The Lehrers said the child provoked the dog and that while protecting himself, Taro scratched her lip. Taro had never before hurt a human being, but he had been in three dogfights and had killed a dog during one of the fights. A panel of local authorities ruled that Taro fell under the state's vicious-dog law and sentenced the Akita to death. A three-year legal nightmare ensued as the Lehrers fought their way through municipal court, superior court, a state appeals court, and finally the New Jersey Supreme Court. While the legal battle raged on, Taro remained on death row at Bergen County Jail in Hackensack, where he was kept in a climate-controlled cell and was allowed two exercise walks a day. By the time his execution day neared, the dog had become an international celebrity. Animal rights activist and former actress Brigitte Bardot pleaded for clemency; a businessman from Kenya raised money to save the dog. Thousands of animal lovers wrote to the Lehrers and offered to adopt the dog. Even the dog's jailer and the assemblyman behind the vicious-dog law interceded on behalf of Taro. But when the courts failed to free the dog, the final verdict fell to Governor Christine Todd Whitman. Although the governor did not exactly pardon the Akita, she agreed to release him on three conditions: Taro would be exiled from New Jersey; Taro must have new owners; Taro's new owners, or the Lehrers, must assume all financial liability for the dog's future actions. The Lehrers agreed, and the dog was released in February 1994, after spending three years in jail. The Lehrers subsequently found a new home for Taro in Pleasantville, New York. When all the costs of the canine death-row case were added up, the total exceeded $100,000. Taro died of natural causes in 1999.

— A.W. & C.O.M.

The 7 Wonders of the Ancient World

Who created one of the earliest and most enduring of all lists, a list that arbitrarily named the seven most spectacular sights existing in the world 150 years before the birth of Jesus Christ? The list was created by a most respected Byzantine mathematician and traveller named Philon. In a series of arduous trips, Philon saw all of the Western civilised world there was to see in his time, and then he sat down and wrote a short but widely circulated paper entitled *De Septem Orbis Spectaculis* (The Seven Wonders of the World).

1. The Great Pyramid of Cheops (Egypt)

Begun as a royal tomb in c. 2600BC, standing in splendour 2,000 years before any of the other Seven Wonders were built, this largest of Egypt's 80-odd pyramids is the only Wonder to have survived to this day. Located outside Cairo, near Giza, the burial tomb of King Cheops was made up of 2.3 million blocks of stone, some of them 2½ tons in weight. The height is 481 ft, the width at the base 755 ft on each side, large enough to enclose London's Westminster Abbey, Rome's St Peter's and Milan's and Florence's main cathedrals.

2. The Hanging Gardens of Babylon (Iraq)

They were not hanging gardens, but gardens on balconies or terraces. When Nebuchadnezzar brought home his new wife, a princess from Medes, she pined for the mountains and lush growth of her native land. To please her, in 600BC the king started to build a man-made mountain with exotic growths. Actually it was a square climbing upward, each densely planted with grass, flowers and fruit trees, irrigated from below by pumps manned by slaves or oxen. Inside and beneath the gardens, the queen held court amid the vegetation and artificial rain. Due to the erosion of time and influx of conquerors, the Hanging Gardens had been levelled and reduced to wilderness when Pliny the Elder visited them before his death in AD79.

3. The Statue of Zeus at Olympia (Greece)

The multicoloured Temple of Zeus, in the area where the Greek Olympic Games were held every fourth year, contained the magnificent statue of Zeus, king of the gods. Sculptured by Phidias (who had done Athena for the Parthenon) some time after 432BC, the statue was 40 ft high, made of ivory and gold plates set on wood. Zeus, with jewels for eyes, sat on a golden throne, feet resting on a footstool of gold. Ancients came from afar to worship at the god's feet. A Greek writer, Pausanias, saw the statue intact as late as the second century AD. After that it disappeared from history, probably the victim of looting armies and fire.

4. The Temple of Diana at Ephesus (Turkey)

Summing up his Seven Wonders, Philon chose his favourite: 'But when I saw the temple at Ephesus rising to the clouds, all these other wonders were put in the shade.' The temple, a religious shrine built after 350BC, housed a statue of Diana, goddess of hunting, symbol of fertility. The kings of many Asian states contributed to the construction. The temple, 225 ft wide and 525 ft long, was supported by 127 marble columns 60 ft high. St Paul, in the New Testament, railed against it, being quoted as saying that 'the temple of the great goddess Diana should be despised, and her magnificence should be destroyed, whom all Asia and the world worshippeth'. The craftsmen of the temple disagreed: 'And when they heard these sayings, they were full of wrath, and cried out saying, "Great is Diana of the Ephesians"'. Ravaged and brought down by invaders, the temple was rebuilt three times before the Goths permanently destroyed it in AD262. In 1874, after 11 years of digging, the English archaeologist J.T. Wood unearthed fragments of the original columns.

5. The Tomb of King Mausolus at Halicarnassus (Turkey)

King Mausolus, conqueror of Rhodes, ruled over the Persian province of Caria. His queen, Artemisia, was also his sister.

When he died in 353BC, he was cremated and his grieving widow drank his ashes in wine. As a memorial to him, she determined to build the most beautiful tomb in the world at Halicarnassus, now called Bodrum. She sent to Greece for the greatest architects and sculptors, and by 350BC the memorial was complete. There was a rectangular sculptured marble tomb on a platform, then 36 golden-white Ionic columns upon which sat an architrave, which in turn held a pyramid topped by a bronzed chariot with statues of Mausolus and Artemisia. The monument survived 1,500 years, only to tumble down in an earthquake. What remains of it today is the word 'mausoleum'.

6. The Colossus of Rhodes on the Isle of Rhodes (in the Aegean Sea)

To celebrate being saved from a Macedonian siege by Ptolemy I, the Rhodians, between 292 and 280BC, erected a mammoth statue to their heavenly protector, the sun-god Apollo. Chares, who had studied under a favourite of Alexander the Great, fashioned the statue. The nude Colossus was

120 ft tall, with its chest and back 60 ft around, built of stone blocks and iron and plated with thin bronze. It did not stand astride the harbour, with room for ships to pass between the legs, but stood with feet together on a promontory at the entrance to the harbour. In 224 BC it was felled by an earthquake. It lay in ruins for almost 900 years. In AD 667 the Arabs, who controlled Rhodes, sold the 720,900 lb of broken statue for scrap metal to a Jewish merchant. When the merchant hauled his purchase to Alexandria, he found that it required 900 camel loads.

7. The Lighthouse on the Isle of Pharos (off Alexandria, Egypt)

On orders of Ptolemy Philadelphus, in 200 BC, the architect Sostratus of Cnidus constructed a pharos or lighthouse such as the world had not seen before. Built on a small island off Alexandria, the tiers of the marble tower – first square, then round, each with a balcony – rose to a height of 400 ft. At the summit a huge brazier with an eternal flame was amplified by a great glass mirror so that the fire could be seen

300 miles out at sea. Half the lighthouse was torn down by occupying Arabs, who hoped to find gold inside the structure. The rest of the structure crashed to the ground when an earthquake struck in 1375.

– I.W.

23 Cases of Bizarre Weather

1. New England's Dark Day

The sun did rise in New England on May 19, 1780, but by midday the sky had turned so dark that it was almost impossible to read or conduct business, and lunch had to be served by candlelight. The phenomenon was noted as far north as Portland, Maine, and as far south as northern New Jersey. General George Washington made mention of the spectacle in his diary. At Hartford, Connecticut, there was great fear that the Day of Judgement had arrived, and at the state legislature a motion was made to adjourn. Calmer heads prevailed and when the sky cleared the following day, it was generally concluded that the problem had been caused by smoke and ash from a fire 'out West'.

2. Thunder and Lightning During Snowstorm

During the night of February 13, 1853, the residents of Mt Desert Island, Maine, were frightened by the freak attack of a thunderstorm during a snowstorm. Bolts of purple lightning flashed to the ground and balls of fire entered homes, injuring several people. Fortunately, no one was killed.

3. Giant Snowflakes

Huge snowflakes, 15 in. across and 8 in. thick, fell on the Coleman ranch at Fort Keogh, Montana, on January 28, 1887. The size of the flakes, which were described as being 'bigger than milk pans', was verified by a mail carrier who was caught in the storm.

4. Turtle Hail

Included in a severe hailstorm in Mississippi on May 11, 1894, was a 6-in.-by-8-in. gopher turtle, which fell to the ground, completely encased in ice, at Bovina, east of Vicksburg.

5. Sudden Temperature Rise

On February 21, 1918, the temperature in Granville, North Dakota, rose 83° Fahrenheit in 12 hours – from -33° Fahrenheit (-36.3° Celsius) in the early morning to 50° Fahrenheit (10° Celsius) in the late afternoon.

6. Fourth of July Blizzard

Patriotic celebrants were stunned in 1918 when a major blizzard swept across the western plains of the United States, disrupting Fourth of July festivities in several states. Independence Day began with the usual picnics and parties, but in the afternoon the temperature dropped suddenly and rain began to fall, followed by hail, snow and gale-force winds.

7. Heaviest Snowfall

On April 5 and 6, 1969, 68 in. (172.7 cm) of snow fell on Bessans, France, in only 19 hours.

8. Slowest Hail

On April 24, 1930, at 2.30 p.m., hail began to fall at Hinaidi, Iraq, at the remarkably slow speed of 9 mph. A clever observer was able to determine the speed by timing the fall of several specimens against the side of a building.

9. Greatest Temperature Fluctuation

The most bizarre temperature changes in history occurred at Spearfish, South Dakota, on January 22, 1943. At 7.30 a.m. the thermometer read -4° Fahrenheit. However, by 7.32 a.m. the temperature had risen 45°, to 49° Fahrenheit. By 9.00 a.m. the temperature had drifted up to 54° Fahrenheit. Then, suddenly, it began to plunge, 58° in 27 minutes, until, at 9.27 a.m., it had returned to -4° Fahrenheit.

10. Most Rain in One Minute

The most rain ever recorded in one minute was 1½ in. (2.68 cm) at Barot on the Caribbean island of Guadeloupe on November 26, 1970.

11. Curious Precipitation at the Empire State Building

While rain was falling in the street in front of the Empire State Building on November 3, 1958, guards near the top of the building were making snowballs.

12. Point Rainfall

An extreme case of localised rainfall occurred the night of August 2, 1966, one-and-a-half miles northeast of Greenfield, New Hampshire. Robert H. Stanley reported that rain began to fall at 7.00 p.m., reaching great intensity from 7.45 p.m. until 10.15 p.m. When he awoke the next morning, Mr Stanley found that his rain gauge had filled to the 5.75-in. (14.6 cm) mark. However, Stanley's neighbour three-tenths of a mile (483 m.) away had collected only one-half in. (1.27 cm) in his rain gauge. Walking around the area, Stanley discovered that the heavy rainfall was limited to no more than one half-mile (805 m.) in any direction. Another strange case of point rainfall took place on November 11, 1958, in the backyard of Mrs R. Babington of Alexandria, Louisiana. Although there were no clouds in the sky, a misty drizzle fell over an area of

100 sq. ft (9.3 sq. m.) for two and a half hours. Mrs Babington called a local reporter, who confirmed the phenomenon. The Shreveport weather bureau suggested the moisture had been formed by condensation from a nearby air conditioner, but their theory was never proved.

13. Snow in Miami

At 6.10 a.m. on January 19, 1977 West Palm Beach reported its first snowfall ever. By 8.30 a.m. snow was falling in Fort Lauderdale, the furthest south that snow had ever been reported in Florida. The snow continued south to Miami, and some even fell in Homestead, 23 miles south of Miami International Airport. The cold wave was so unusual that heat lamps had to be brought out to protect the iguanas at Miami's Crandon Park Zoo.

14. Highest Temperature

On September 13, 1922 the temperature in Azizia, Libya, reached 136.4° Fahrenheit (58° Celsius) – in the shade.

15. Lowest Temperature

On July 21, 1983 the thermometer at Vostok, Antarctica, registered minus 128.6° Fahrenheit (-89.2° Celsius). Vostok also holds the record for consistently cold weather. To reach an optimum temperature of 65° Fahrenheit (18.3° Celsius), Vostok would require 48,800 'heating degree days' a year. By comparison, Fairbanks, Alaska, needs only 14,300.

16. Extreme Temperatures

Temperatures in Verkhoyansk, Russia, have ranged from 98° Fahrenheit (37° Celsius) down to 90.4° Fahrenheit (-68° Celsius), a variance of 188.4° Fahrenheit (105° Celsius).

17. Longest Hot Spell

Marble Bar, Western Australia, experienced 160 consecutive days of 100° Fahrenheit (37.8° Celsius) temperatures from October 31, 1923 to April 7, 1924.

18. The Rainiest Day

On March 16, 1952, 73.62 in. (187 cm) of rain – more than 6 ft – fell at Cilaos on Réunion Island east of Madagascar. Another 24 in. (60.96 cm) fell during the 24 hours surrounding March 16.

19. Most Rain in 15 Days

Cherrapunji, Assam, India, received 189 in. (226.06 cm) of rain between June 24 and July 8, 1931. Back in 1861, Cherrapunji received 366.14 in. (930 cm) of rain in one month and 905.12 in. (2,400 cm) for the calendar year.

20. No Rain

The driest place on Earth is Arica, Chile, in the Atacama Desert. No rain fell there for more than 14 years, between October 1903 and December 1917. Over a 59-year period, Arica averaged three-hundredths of an inch (.76 mm) of rain a year.

21. Snowiest Day

The largest snowfall in a 24-hour period was 75.8 in. (192.5 cm) – more than 6 ft – recorded at Silver Lake, Colorado, on April 14–15, 1921.

22. Snowiest Season

Paradise Ranger Station on Mt Rainier in Washington State recorded 1,122 in. (2,850 cm) of snow in 1971–72. Their average is 582 in. (1,478 cm).

23. Champion Hurricane

Hurricane John, which flourished in August and September of 1994, was notable for two reasons. It lasted for all or part of 31 days, making it the longest-lived tropical storm on record. It also crossed over the International Date Line twice, changing its name from Hurricane John to Typhoon John and back to Hurricane John.

28 Bad Reviews of Famous Works

1. *The Monkey Wrench Gang* – Edward Abbey, 1975
The author of this book should be neutered and locked away
forever. – *San Juan County Record*

2. *Les Fleurs Du Mal* – Charles Baudelaire, 1857
In a hundred years the history of French literature will only
mention [this work] as a curio. – Emile Zola, in *Emile Zola*,
1953.

**3. *Malloy; Malone Dies; The Unnameable* – Samuel
Beckett, 1959 (three novels in one volume)**
The suggestion that something larger is being said about the
human predicament . . . won't hold water, any more than
Beckett's incontinent heroes can. – *The Spectator*

4. *Naked Lunch* – William S. Burroughs, 1963

. . . the merest trash, not worth a second look. – *New Republic*

5. *In Cold Blood* – Truman Capote, 1965

One can say of this book – with sufficient truth to make it worth saying: 'This isn't writing. It's research.' – Stanley Kauffmann, *New Republic*

6. *The Deerslayer* – James Fenimore Cooper, 1841

In one place *Deerslayer*, and in the restricted space of two-thirds of a page, Cooper has scored 114 offences against literary art out of a possible 115. It breaks the record. – Mark Twain, *How to Tell a Story and Other Essays*, 1897

7. *An American Tragedy* – Theodore Dreiser, 1925

His style, if style it may be called, is offensively colloquial, commonplace and vulgar. – *Boston Evening Transcript*

8. *Absalom, Absalom!* – William Faulkner, 1936

The final blowup of what was once a remarkable, if minor, talent. – Clifton Fadiman, *New Yorker*

9. *The Great Gatsby* – F. Scott Fitzgerald, 1925

What has never been alive cannot very well go on living. So this is a book of the season only . . . – *New York Herald Tribune*

10. *Madame Bovary* – Gustave Flaubert, 1857

Monsieur Flaubert is not a writer. – *Le Figaro*

11. *The Recognitions* – William Gaddis, 1955

The Recognitions is an evil book, a scurrilous book, a profane, a scatalogical book and an exasperating book . . . what this squalling overwritten book needs above all is to have its mouth washed out with lye soap. – *Chicago Sun Times*

12. *Catch-22* – Joseph Heller, 1961

Heller wallows in his own laughter . . . and the sort of antic behaviour the children fall into when they know they are losing our attention. – Whitey Balliett, *New Yorker*

13. *The Sun Also Rises* – Ernest Hemingway, 1926

His characters are as shallow as the saucers in which they stack their daily emotions . . . – *The Dial*

14. *For Whom the Bell Tolls* – Ernest Hemingway, 1940

This book offers not pleasure but mounting pain . . . – *Catholic World*

15. *Brave New World* – Aldous Huxley, 1932

A lugubrious and heavy-handed piece of propaganda. – *New York Herald Tribune*

16. *Lives of the English Poets* – Samuel Johnson, 1779–81

Johnson wrote the lives of the poets and left out the poets. – Elizabeth Barrett Browning, *The Book of the Poets*, 1842

17. *Finnegans Wake* – James Joyce, 1939

As one tortures one's way through *Finnegans Wake* an impression grows that Joyce has lost his hold on human life. – Alfred Kazin, *New York Herald Tribune*

18. *Babbit* – Sinclair Lewis, 1929

As a humorist, Mr Lewis makes valiant attempts to be funny; he merely succeeds in being silly. – *Boston Evening Transcript*

19. *Lolita* – Vladimir Nabokov, 1958

. . . Any bookseller should be very sure that he knows in advance that he is selling very literate pornography. – *Kirkus Reviews*

20. *The Moviegoer* – Walker Percy, 1961

Mr Percy's prose needs oil and a good checkup. – *New Yorker*

21. *A Midsummer Night's Dream* – William Shakespeare, performed in London, 1662

The most stupid ridiculous play that I ever saw in my life. – Samuel Pepys, *Diary*

22. *Hamlet* – William Shakespeare, 1601

One would imagine this piece to be the work of a drunken savage. – Voltaire (1768), in *The Works of M. de Voltaire*, 1901

23. *Gulliver's Travels* – Jonathan Swift, 1726

. . . evidence of a diseased mind and lacerated heart. – John Dunlop, *The History of Fiction*, 1814

24. *Anna Karenina* – Leo Tolstoy, 1877

Sentimental rubbish . . . Show me one page that contains an idea. – *The Odessa Courier*

25. *Breakfast of Champions* – Kurt Vonnegut, 1973

From time to time it's nice to have a book you can hate – it clears the pipes – and I hate this book. – Peter Prescott, *Newsweek*

26. *Leaves of Grass* – Walt Whitman, 1855

Whitman is as unacquainted with art as a hog is with mathematics. – *The London Critic*

27. *The Waves* – Virginia Woolf, 1931

The book is dull. – H.C. Hardwood, *Saturday Review of Literature*

28. *A Dictionary of the English Language* – Samuel Johnson, 1755

. . . the confidence now reposed in its accuracy is the greatest injury to philology that now exists – Noah Webster, letter, 1807

17 Pairs of Contradictory Proverbs

1. Look before you leap.
   He who hesitates is lost.

2. If at first you don't succeed, try, try again.
   Don't beat your head against a brick wall.

3. Absence makes the heart grow fonder.
   Out of sight, out of mind.

4. Never put off until tomorrow what you can do today.
   Don't cross the bridge until you come to it.

5. Two heads are better than one.
Paddle your own canoe.

6. More haste, less speed.
Time waits for no man.

7. You're never too old to learn.
You can't teach an old dog new tricks.

8. A word to the wise is sufficient.
Talk is cheap.

9. It's better to be safe than sorry.
Nothing ventured, nothing gained.

10. Don't look a gift horse in the mouth.
Beware of Greeks bearing gifts.

11. Do unto others as you would have others do unto you.
Nice guys finish last.

12. Hitch your wagon to a star.
   Don't bite off more than you can chew.

13. Many hands make light work.
   Too many cooks spoil the broth.

14. Don't judge a book by its cover.
   Clothes make the man.

15. The squeaking wheel gets the grease.
   Silence is golden.

16. Birds of a feather flock together.
   Opposites attract.

17. The pen is mightier than the sword.
   Actions speak louder than words.

— J.Ba.

So To Speak – The Truth About 16 Common Sayings

1. At a Snail's Pace

The fastest land snail on record is a garden snail named Archie, who won the 1995 World Snail Racing Championship in Longhan, England, by covering 13 inches in 2 minutes. Archie's pace was .0062 mph.

2. Just a Moment

According to an old English time unit, a moment takes $1\frac{1}{2}$ minutes. In medieval times, a moment was either $\frac{1}{40}$ or $\frac{1}{50}$ of an hour, but by rabbinical reckoning a moment is precisely $\frac{1}{1,080}$ of an hour.

3. All the Tea in China

The United Nations Food and Agricultural Organisation estimates that all the tea in China in 2003 amounted to 800,345 metric tons.

4. By a Hair's Breadth

Although the breadth of a hair varies from head to head, the dictionary definition of hair's breadth is $1/48$ in.

5. Only Skin-deep

The depth of human skin ranges from $1/100$ in. on the eyelid to $1/5$ in. on the back.

6. Eats Like a Horse

A 1,200-lb horse eats about 15 lb of hay and 9 lb of grain each day. This amounts to $1/50$ of its own weight each day, or 7 times its own weight each year. The real gluttons in the animal kingdom are birds, who consume more than 90 times their own weight in food each year.

7. A Picture is Worth a Thousand Words

The amount paid by magazines for photographs and for written articles varies widely. Both *Travel & Leisure* magazine and *Harper's* magazine pay an average of $350 for a photograph and $1 a word for articles. Based on this scale, a picture is worth 350 words. When *The Book of Lists* first studied this matter in 1978, a picture was worth 2000 words.

8. Quick as a Wink

The average wink, or corneal reflex blink, lasts $1/10$ sec.

9. Quicker Than You Can Say 'Jack Robinson'

When members of *The Book of Lists* staff were asked to say 'Jack Robinson', their speed varied from $1/2$ to 1 sec. It is acknowledged that this may not be a representative sample of the world population.

10. Selling Like Hot Cakes

Sales figures for the International House of Pancakes show that their 1,164 US restaurants sold a total of 700,000,000 pancakes in 2003.

11. Since Time Immemorial

Time immemorial is commonly defined as beyond the memory of any living person, or a time extending so far back as to be indefinite. However, for the purposes of English law, a statute passed in 1275 decreed that time immemorial was any point in time prior to 1189 – the year when Richard I began his reign.

12. Knee-high to a Grasshopper

According to Charles L. Hogue of the Los Angeles County Museum of Natural History, this figure necessarily depends upon the size of the grasshopper. For the average grasshopper, the knee-high measurement would be about $\frac{1}{2}$ in.

13. High as a Kite

The record for the greatest height attained by a single kite on a single line is 14,509 feet. The kite was flown by a group headed by Richard Synergy at Kincardine, Ontario, Canada, on August 12, 2000.

14. Faster than a Speeding Bullet

The fastest bullet is a calibre .50 Saboted Light Armor Penetrator-Tracer M962. Used in M2 machine guns, it travels 4,000 feet (.75 mile) per second. The fastest non-military bullet is the .257 Weatherby Spire Point, which travels 3,825 ft (.72 mile) per second.

15. Blood is Thicker than Water

In chemistry, water is given a specific gravity, or relative density, of 1.00, because it is used as the standard against which all other densities are measured. By comparison, blood has a specific gravity of 1.06 – only slightly thicker than water.

16. A King's Ransom

The largest king's ransom in history was raised by Richard the Lionheart to obtain his release from the Holy Roman Emperor Henry VI in 1194. The English people were forced to contribute almost 150,000 marks to free their sovereign. Nearly as large a ransom was raised by Atahualpa, King of the Incas, when he offered Pizarro a roomful of gold and two roomfuls of silver for his release in 1532. At today's prices, the ransom would be worth more than £4 million (or $7 million). Unfortunately, it was not sufficient to buy Atahualpa his freedom; he was given a mock trial and executed.

4 Unfortunate Product Names and I Honourable Mention

PINTO

A corporate or product name can symbolise more than intended, especially when that name is used in other lands. Today's multinational markets require sensitivity to other cultures, as many companies have learned the hard way.

1. Gros Jos

Hunt-Wesson introduced its Big John products in Canada before realising that the name, which translated to *Gros Jos*, was French-Canadian slang for 'big breasts'. However, sales did not suffer from this translation.

2. Pinto

The Ford Pinto suffered image problems when it went on sale in Brazil – pinto is Portuguese slang for 'small male genitals'. For Brazilian buyers, Ford changed the name to Corcel, which means 'horse'.

3. Bite the Wax Tadpole

When Coca-Cola expanded into China in the 1920s, the company chose Chinese characters which, when pronounced, would sound like the English name for the drink. Those particular Chinese letters, though, actually translated to 'bite the wax tadpole' or 'wax-flattened mare'. The company now uses characters that mean 'good mouth, good pleasure' or 'happiness in the mouth'.

4. Pledge

The Johnson Company retained the American name of the wax product when it was introduced in the Netherlands. Unfortunately, in Dutch it means 'piss', making it difficult for shoppers to ask for Pledge. The product survived because most Dutch retail stores converted to self-service.

HONOURABLE MENTION

The Yokohama Rubber Company was forced to withdraw hundreds of tyres from the sultanate of Brunei when Islamic authorities complained that the tread design resembled the word for Allah.

29 Words
Rarely Used in Their
Positive Form

Negative Form	Positive Form
1. *Inadvertent*	Advertent (giving attention; heedful)
2. *Analgesia*	Algesia (sensitiveness to pain)
3. *Antibiotic*	Biotic (of or relating to life)
4. *Unconscionable*	Conscionable (conscientious)
5. *Disconsolate*	Consolate (consoled, comforted)
6. *Incorrigible*	Corrigible (correctable)
7. *Uncouth*	Couth (marked by finesse, polish, etc; smooth)
8. *Indelible*	Delible (capable of being deleted)
9. *Nondescript*	Descript (described; inscribed)
10. *Indomitable*	Domitable (tamable)

11.	*Ineffable*	Effable (capable of being uttered or expressed)
12.	*Inevitable*	Evitable (avoidable)
13.	*Feckless*	Feckful (effective; sturdy; powerful)
14.	*Unfurl*	Furl (to draw in and secure to a staff)
15.	*Disgruntle*	Gruntle (to put in good humour)
16.	*Disgust*	Gust (inclination; liking)
17.	*Antihistamine*	Histamine (a crystalline base that is held to be responsible for the dilation and increased permeability of blood vessels which play a major role in allergic reactions)
18.	*Disinfectant*	Infectant (an agent of infection)
19.	*Illicit*	Licit (not forbidden by law; allowable)
20.	*Immaculate*	Maculate (marked with spots; besmirched)
21.	*Innocuous*	Nocuous (likely to cause injury; harmful)
22.	*Deodorant*	Odorant (an odorous substance)
23.	*Impeccable*	Peccable (liable or prone to sin)

24.	*Impervious*	Pervious (being of a substance that can be penetrated or permeated)
25.	*Implacable*	Placable (of a tolerant nature; tractable)
26.	*Ruthless*	Ruthful (full of compassion or pity)
27.	*Insipid*	Sipid (affecting the organs of taste; savoury)
28.	*Unspeakable*	Speakable (capable of being spoken of)
29.	*Unwieldy*	Wieldy (strong; manageable)

— R.A.

18 Untranslatable Words

Here are 18 words and phrases that have no equivalent in English; edited by the *Book of Lists* authors from Howard Rheingold's *They Have A Word For It*, published by Sarabande.

1. Cavoli riscadati (Italian)

The attempt to revive a dead love affair. Literally, 'reheated cabbage'. The result of such a culinary effort is usually unworkable, messy and distasteful.

2. Dohada (Sanskrit)

Unusual appetites and cravings of pregnant women. Dohada is a word older than the English language. There is a scientific basis for dohada: women who want to eat dirt (a condition called pica) or chalk, are attempting to ingest essential minerals.

3. Drachenfutter (German)

A gift brought home from a husband to his wife after he has stayed out late. Literally, 'dragon fodder'. In decades past, men went to bars on Saturday night with the wrapped gifts prepared in advance. This word can also be used for all gifts or acts performed out of guilt for having too much fun, such as gifts from employees to bosses, children to parents, students to teachers, and so on.

4. Esprit de l'escalier (French)

The brilliantly witty response to a public insult that comes into your mind only after you have left the party. Literally, 'the spirit of the staircase'. Observes author Rheingold, 'Sometimes, this feeling about what you ought to have said at a crucial moment can haunt you for the rest of your life.'

5. Kyoikumama (Japanese)

A mother who pushes her children into academic achievement. A derogatory term that literally means 'education mama'. The pressure on Japanese students is severe and

intense – but they are hardly the only victims of parental push-
ing. The American fad for using flashcards and the like, to
create infant prodigies, is practised by fathers and mothers.

6. Nakhes (Yiddish)

A mixture of pleasure and pride, particularly the kind that a
parent gets from a child. It is something one relishes, as in
'May you only get nakhes from your son!'

7. Ondinnonk (Iroquoian)

This is a noun which describes the soul's innermost desires;
the angelic parts of human nature. Listening to one's inner
instinct to perform a kindly act is to let our ondinnonk be our
guide.

8. Razbliuto (Russian)

The feeling a person has for someone he once loved but now
does not. In the original Russian it applies to a man, but has
become applicable for both sexes.

9. Schadenfreude (German)

The literal translation is 'joy in damage'. It is the pleasure one feels as a result of someone else's misfortune, like seeing a rival slip on a banana peel. Schadenfreude is not as strong as taking revenge, because it's a thought or a feeling, not an action. But when your noisy neighbour's car breaks down, and you're secretly pleased – that's schadenfreude.

10. Tartle (Scottish)

To hesitate in recognising a person or thing, as happens when you are introduced to someone whose name you cannot recall. A way out of this social gaffe is to say, 'Pardon my sudden tartle!'

11. Palayi (Bantu)

A mythical monster that scratches at the door. The very same 'monster' haunts the doors of South Carolina, America and West Africa.

12. Katzenjammer (German)

A monumentally severe hangover. The inspiration for the early American comic strip 'The Katzenjammer Kids'. On New Year's Eve, it is common for one German to remark to another, 'You're setting yourself up for a real Katzenjammer.' (The party in question may require some 'Drachenfutter'.)

13. Qualunquismo (Italian)

This describes an attitude of indifference to political and social issues. It is derived from a satirical political journal called *L'uomo qualunque*: the man in the street. For example, a great many people believe that the US president is elected by a majority of qualified voters. In fact, only 29% of all voters led to Ronald Reagan's 'landslide victory' in 1984.

14. Bilita mpash (Bantu)

This denotes blissful dreams. In English we have nightmares, but no word for waking feeling happy. In Bantu, the word is further defined as a 'legendary, blissful state where all is forgiven and forgotten'. The African-American equivalent for bilita mpash is a 'beluthathatchee', believed to be traced to African-American slang from its Bantu roots.

15. Zalatwic (Polish)

Zalatwic means using acquaintances to accomplish things unofficially. It means going around the system to trade, to evade exchanges in cash. Since shortages seem to be a fact of social life, these exchanges can range from the profound (a new apartment) to the menial (a new pair of trainers).

16. Hari kuyo (Japanese)

A hari kuyo is a shrine for broken sewing needles. In Japan's Wakayama Province, every village has a shrine where a periodic service is performed for the broken needles. The belief is that the sewing needles worked hard all their lives and died in the service of those who used them. When they break, they are put to rest on a soft bed of tofu.

17. Salogok (Eskimo)

Salogok is young black ice. It is a famous fact that Eskimos have 17 different words for kinds of snow. In *Hunters of the Northern Ice*, a book by Richard K. Nelson, there is an appendix on Eskimo ice-words, titled 'Eskimo Sea-Ice Terminology'. A sample from this work is 'Salogok: nilas, or black young ice: a thin, flexible sheet of newly formed ice which will not support a man, is weak enough to enable seals to break through it with their heads to breathe, and breaks through with one firm thrust of the unaak.'

18. Biritululo (Kiriwana, New Guinea)

Comparing yams to settle disputes. In New Guinean culture nobody discusses what everybody knows concerning sensitive subjects. Breaking this code of polite behaviour results in violent disputes. Yet yams are so important in Kiriwana, that people boast about their own yams, to the point of starting a fight. Settling this fight calms everyone down.

– By permission of the author, Howard Rheingold

16 Cases of People Killed by God

1. Entire World Population Except Noah and Seven Relatives (Genesis 6, 7)

Transgression: Violence, corruption and generalised wickedness.

Method of execution: Flood.

2. Entire Populations of Sodom and Gomorrah Except Lot, His Wife and their Two Daughters (Genesis 19)

Transgression: Widespread wickedness and lack of respect for the deity.

Method of execution: Rain of fire and brimstone.

3. Lot's Wife (Genesis 19)

Transgression: Looked back.

Method of execution: Turned into a pillar of salt.

4. Er (Genesis 38)

Transgression: Wickedness.
Method of execution: Unknown.

5. Onan (Genesis 38)

Transgression: Refused to make love to his brother Er's widow.
Method of execution: Unknown.

6. All the Firstborn of Egypt (Exodus 12)

Transgression: Egypt was cruel to the Jews.
Method of execution: Unknown.

7. Pharaoh and the Egyptian Army (Exodus 14)

Transgression: Pursued the Jews.
Method of execution: Drowned.

8. Nadab and Abihu (Leviticus 10)

Transgression: Offered strange fire.
Method of execution: Fire.

9. Korah, Dathan, Abiram and Their Families (Numbers 16)

Transgression: Rejected authority of Moses and started own congregation.

Method of execution: Swallowed by earth.

10. 250 Followers of Korah (Numbers 16)

Transgression: Supported Korah.

Method of execution: Fire.

11. 14,700 Israelites (Numbers 16)

Transgression: Murmured against Moses and his brother Aaron following execution of Korah and his supporters.

Method of execution: Plague.

12. Unknown Number of Retreating Amorite Soldiers (Joshua 10)

Transgression: Fought the Israelites.

Method of execution: Hailstones.

13. Uzzah (2 Samuel 6)

Transgression: Touched the ark of God after oxen shook it while pulling it on a cart.

Method of execution: Unknown.

14. 70,000 People (2 Samuel 24)

Transgression: King David ordered a census of the population.

Method of execution: Plague.

15. 102 Soldiers of King Ahaziah (2 Kings 1)

Transgression: Tried to capture Elijah the Tishbite.

Method of execution: Fire.

16. Ananias and Sapphira (Acts 5)

Transgression: Land fraud.

Method of execution: Unknown.

17 Health Experts and How They Died

1. Stuart M. Berger (1953–94)

Age at death: 40

The 6 ft 7 in. Berger successfully reduced his weight from 420 to 210 lb. He described his techniques in such bestsellers as *The Southampton Diet* (1984) and *Dr Berger's Immune Power Diet* (1986). Berger claimed that his diet would boost the immune system and promote longevity. He died in his New York City apartment from a heart attack brought on by cocaine abuse and obesity: at the time of his death he weighed 365 lb.

2. Sylvester Graham (1794–1851)

Age at death: 57

A clergyman and temperance leader, Graham believed that good health could be achieved through a strict regime which included cold showers, daily exercise and a vegetarian diet. In 1847 he spoke to an audience in Boston and triggered a near riot by butchers and bakers who were angered by his advocacy of vegetarianism and homemade bread. He was deeply shaken by the attack and his health began to decline. Treatment with stimulants, mineral water and tepid baths proved to be of no lasting help, and he died broken in body and spirit. He is remembered today chiefly for his creation of the Graham cracker, though the present-day commercial product – containing bleached flour, sugar and preservatives – would have horrified him.

3. Eugene Sandow (1867–1925)

Age at death: 58

Through the application of scientific methods of muscle development, Sandow transformed himself from a weak youth into the 'world's strongest man', as showbusiness promoter Florenz Ziegfeld billed him at the 1893 World's Columbian Exposition in Chicago. In 1911 Sandow was appointed professor of physical culture to King George V. However, Sandow's primary concern was to convince the average man that anyone could achieve strength and vigour by exercising for a little as 20 minutes a day. The strong man pushed himself beyond even his immense capacities when, without any assistance, he lifted a car out of a ditch after an accident. He suffered a severe strain and died soon afterward from a burst blood vessel in the brain. However, some believe that he actually died of syphilis.

4. Émile Coué (1857–1926)

Age at death: 69

Trained as a pharmacist, Coué became interested in hypnotism and developed a health treatment based on autosuggestion. He told his patients that their health would improve dramatically if, morning and evening, they would repeat faithfully: 'Every day and in every way, I am becoming better and better.' Prior to WWI, an estimated 40,000 patients flocked to his clinic each year and Coué claimed a 97% success rate. Coué kept up a demanding schedule. After one of his lecture tours he returned to his home in Nancy, France, and complained of exhaustion. He died there of heart failure.

5. Nathan Pritikin (1915–85)

Age at death: 69

Pritikin was diagnosed with heart disease in his mid-40s. Although he did not have a background in medicine, he spent the next 20 years researching diet and nutrition. He developed a low-fat, low-cholesterol and high-fibre diet that he credited with reversing his heart disease. In 1976 he opened the Pritikin Longevity Center in California to spread the word. He also published eight books on diet and exercise. His programme gained credibility in 1984 when the National Institutes of Health concluded that lowering cholesterol reduced the risk of heart disease. Unfortunately, at the same time, Pritikin developed leukaemia. The chemotherapy that he underwent to fight the cancer brought about anaemia, kidney failure and severe pain. On February 21, 1985, Pritikin committed suicide in his hospital bed by slashing his wrists with a razor. The leukaemia had probably been caused by a dubious medical technique that Pritikin underwent in 1957. His doctor had prescribed a series of X-ray treatments to destroy a fungal infection causing a skin rash. Afterwards,

Pritikin was diagnosed with an elevated white blood cell count, a frequent precursor to leukaemia.

6. Adelle Davis (1904–74)

Age at death: 70

'You are what you eat,' claimed Davis, the well-known American nutritionist who advocated a natural diet rich in fresh fruits and vegetables along with large doses of vitamins. When she was diagnosed as having bone cancer at the age of 69, her first reaction was disbelief. 'I thought this was for people who drink soft drinks, who eat white bread, who eat refined sugar, and so on,' she said. Eventually she came to accept her illness as a delayed reaction to the 'junk food' eating habits she had acquired in college and which had lasted until the 1950s. Her hope was that those who had faith in her work would not be disheartened by her fatal illness.

7. Max Bircher-Brenner (1867–1939)

Age at death: 71

One of the first exponents of proper nutrition, Bircher-

Brenner advocated the ingestion of raw fruits and vegetables – 'living' food. He also believed that a patient's mind played an important role in the cause of illness and that psychological as well as physical treatment was necessary to cure disease. A premature baby, Bircher-Brenner had been born with a weak heart which doctors said would prevent him from ever living a normal life. Through vigorous physical exercise and careful diet he had attained remarkable health as an adult, but the coronary weakness was not entirely overcome. On January 24, 1939, he died from a ruptured heart vessel.

8. Élie Metchnikoff (1845–1916)

Age at death: 71

Through extensive longevity research the Nobel Prize-winning bacteriologist concluded that the human body was meant to last 100 to 150 years. He became known particularly for his 'Sour Milk Cure', in which he advocated the consumption of yogurt to cleanse the large intestine. In addition, he discovered a bacterium (found only in the intestines of dogs) which he believed could further retard the aging process – and he proceeded to inoculate himself with the microbe. Shortly before his death from heart disease, Metchnikoff detailed in his diary the reasons for his untimely demise: 'intense and precocious activities, fretful character, nervous temperament and tardy start on a sensible regime.'

9. Dr Robert Atkins (1930–2003)

Age at death: 72

On April 17, 2003, the famous 'low-carb diet doctor', Dr Atkins, died after falling on an icy street and hitting his head. It was in 1972 that Atkins – who had a history of heart disease – published the bestselling *Dr Atkins' Diet Revolution*, which advocated consuming meat, eggs and cheese while shunning all carbohydrates, including wheat bread, all rice and fruits. His books sold more than 15 million copies and became the subject of heated debate: other respected dieticians advise the opposite approach – fruit, fresh vegetables and a largely veg-etarian diet. A group of doctors severely critical of Atkins' plan maintain that his programme leads to weight gain and heart disease. Atkins supporters insist that his death was the result of hospitalisation, where, in a coma, he gained 60 lb in fluid retention. Upon entering the hospital, the 6-ft Atkins weighted 195 lb – overweight by the standards of the Center For Heart Disease. He died eight days later at the formidable weight of 265 lb. Defenders of the diet vigorously claim the cause was bloating. His books continue to sell.

10. J.I. Rodale (1898–1971)

Age at death: 72

The head of a multimillion-dollar publishing business, Rodale promulgated his belief in 'organic food' (food free from chemicals and artificial additives) supplemented by natural vitamins through his popular magazines *Organic Gardening* and *Prevention*. He was at the height of his fame when he appeared on *The Dick Cavett Show* on June 9, 1971. After describing the dangers of milk, wheat and sugar, Rodale proceeded to say, 'I'm so healthy that I expect to live on and on.' Shortly after the conclusion of the interview, Rodale slumped in his chair, the victim of a fatal heart attack.

11. Sebastian Kneipp (1821–97)

Age at death: 76

As a young seminary student, Kneipp cured himself of an attack of nervous prostration through hydrotherapy. When he became a priest, he continued his cold-water cures. Eventually he abandoned his priestly duties altogether to give advice to as many as 500 patients a day. The empress of Austria and Pope Leo XIII were among those who consulted him. Kneipp believed that the application of cold water – plus exercise, fresh air, sunshine and walking barefoot over grass and through snow – could cure virtually any mental or physical disorder. An inflammation of his lungs, which had been weak since childhood, resulted in his death.

12. Franz Mesmer (1734–1815)

Age at death: 80

Mesmer believed that a person became ill when his 'animal magnetism' was out of balance. To correct this condition, the Viennese doctor made use of magnets and held séance-like therapeutic sessions for his patients. Hounded out of Vienna on charges of practising magic, Mesmer moved to Paris, where a royal commission (whose members included Benjamin Franklin and Antoine Lavoisier) concluded that Mesmer's 'cures' were due solely to his patients' imaginations. Mesmer was convinced that he would die in his eighty-first year, as a Gypsy woman had foretold. Her prediction came true two months before his eighty-first birthday, when he succumbed to an extremely painful bladder condition that had troubled him for years.

13. D.C. Jarvis (1881–1966)
Age at death: 85

This country doctor became an overnight sensation in 1958 with the publication of *Folk Medicine: A Vermont Doctor's Guide to Good Health*. Part of his appeal derived from the simplicity of his remedies. For example, he suggested that one could stay healthy through a daily dose of two teaspoons each of honey and apple cider vinegar in a glass of water. Jarvis had many supporters, in spite of a Harvard professor's comment that 'This claptrap is strictly for those gullible birds stung by the honey bee.' Jarvis died in a nursing home in Vermont after suffering a cerebral haemorrhage.

14. Bernard MacFadden (1868–1955)

Age at death: 87

Billing himself as a kinestherapist, MacFadden ran a chain of health food restaurants and sanatoria that pushed his programme of exercise, fresh air, personal hygiene and wholesome diet. He also published the popular but controversial magazine *Physical Culture*, which featured photos of men and women posing nearly naked – considered obscene by some in the early twentieth century. Throughout his long life Macfadden was almost always in the news for one reason or another – his marriages, his attacks on the medical establishment, or his founding of a new religion, the Cosmotarian Fellowship. MacFadden celebrated his eighty-third birthday by parachuting 2,500 ft into the Hudson River. The master showman finally succumbed to a urinary tract blockage that he had tried unsuccessfully to combat through fasting.

15. Samuel Hahnemann (1755–1843)

Age at death: 88

A German physician at crosscurrents with the medical beliefs of his day, Hahnemann developed the system of homeopathy. Its basic tenet is that a drug that produces symptoms of illness in a healthy person will cure a sick person who exhibits those symptoms, when that drug is administered in minute doses. Hahnemann died from an inflammation of the bronchial tubes, which had plagued him for 20 years. Although he had come to terms with death ('My earthly shell is worn out,' he stated), his wife was less accepting of the inevitable. She kept his embalmed corpse with her for nine days before giving it up for burial.

16. Mary Baker Eddy (1821–1910)

Age at death: 89

Eddy founded the Christian Science religion after experiencing what she believed to be Christ's method of healing. At the time, she was suffering the effects of a serious fall on the ice. She taught that healing is accomplished not by drugs or medicines but through the affirmation of spiritual truth. Although Eddy enjoyed a remarkably active old age, when her health began to fail she was convinced that it was due to Malicious Animal Magnetism engendered by her enemies. The official verdict was that she died from 'natural causes' after a brief bout of pneumonia. The undertaker who examined the corpse stated: 'I do not remember having found the body of a person of such advanced age in so good a physical condition.'

17. Linus Pauling (1901–94)

Age at death: 93

The only person to win two unshared Nobel Prizes (for Chemistry and Peace, not Medicine), Pauling in 1970 wrote a book arguing that large doses of vitamin C could cure the common cold. Over the years he expanded on his claims, declaring that vitamin C would extend a person's life by decades and ward off cancer and heart disease. Pauling himself took 18,000 mg of vitamin C a day (the recommended daily allowance for adults is 60 mg). Pauling was diagnosed with prostate cancer in December of 1991. He died of complications at his ranch in Big Sur, California, two years later.

— F.B. & C.F.

10 Funguses That Changed History

1. The Yellow Plague (*Aspergillus flavus*)

A. flavus is an innocent-looking but deadly yellowish mould also called aflatoxin. Undoubtedly the cause of countless deaths throughout history, it was not suspected of being poisonous until 1960. That year, a mysterious disease killed 100,000 young turkeys in England and medical researchers traced the 'turkey-X disease' to *A. flavus* growing on the birds' peanut meal feed. Hardy, widespread and lethal, aflatoxin is a powerful liver cancer agent. Even so, people have long cultivated *A. flavus* – in small amounts – as part of the manufacturing process of soy sauce and sake. But *A. flavus* can get out of control easily. It thrives on warm, damp conditions and as it breeds – sometimes to lethal proportions within 24 hours – the mould produces its own heat, which spurs even faster growth. Some of *A. flavus*' favourite dishes are stored peanuts, rice, corn, wheat, potatoes, peas, cocoa, cured hams and sausage.

2. The Mould That Toppled an Industry (*Aspergillus niger*)

This common black mould, most often found on rotting vegetation, played a key role in the collapse of a major industry. Until the early 1920s, Italy produced about 90% of the world's citric acid, using low-grade lemons. Exported mainly to the US as calcium citrate, this citric acid was a costly ingredient – about a dollar a pound – used in food, pharmaceutical and industrial processing. When American chemists discovered that *A. niger*, the most ordinary of moulds, secreted citric acid as it grew in a culture medium, they seized the opportunity to perfect citric-acid production using the easily grown mould. Charles Pfizer & Co., of Brooklyn, New York, became known as the 'world's largest lemon grove' – without a lemon in sight. Hardworking acres of *A. niger* were soon squirting out such quantities of citric acid that by 1923 the price was down to 25 cents per pound and the Italians were out of business.

3. St Anthony's Fire (*Claviceps purpurea*)

A purplish-black, spur-shaped mass, *C. purpurea* is a formidable and even frightening fungus that has long plagued mankind. But in addition to its horrible effects, *C. purpurea* also has valuable medical uses if the greatest care is taken to use tiny amounts. The fungus is a powerful muscle contractor and can control bleeding, speed up childbirth and even induce abortion. It is also the source of the hallucinogenic LSD-25. In doses larger than microscopic, *C. purpurea* – commonly called ergot – produces ergotamine poisoning, a grisly condition known in the Middle Ages as St Anthony's Fire. There is still no cure for this hideous, often fatal disease caused by eating fungus-infected rye. The victim suffers convulsions and performs a frenzied 'dance'. This is often accompanied by a burning sensation in the limbs, which turn gangrenously black and fall off. Some victims of medieval ergotism went insane and many died. In AD994 more than 40,000 people in two French provinces died of ergotism, and in 1722 the powerful fungus forced Peter the Great of Russia to abandon his plan to conquer Turkey when, on the eve of the Battle of Astrakhan, his entire cavalry and 20,000 others were stricken with ergotism. The last recorded outbreak of ergot poisoning was in the French village of Pont-Saint-Esprit in 1951.

4. The Nobel Mould (*Neurospora crassa*)

The humble bread mould *N. crassa* provided the means for scientists to explore the most exciting biological discovery of the twentieth century: DNA. As anyone with an old loaf of bread in the bread box knows, *N. crassa* needs only a simple growing medium and it has a short life cycle. With such cooperative qualities, this reddish mould enabled George Beadle and Edward Tatum to win the Nobel Prize in Medicine/Physiology in 1958 for discovering the role that genes play in passing on hereditary traits from one generation to the next. By X-raying *N. crassa*, the researchers produced mutations of the genes, or components of DNA, and then found which genes corresponded with which traits.

5. The Bluish-green Lifesaver (*Penicillium notatum-chrysogenum*)

A few dots of a rather pretty bluish-green mould were Dr Alexander Fleming's first clue to finding one of the most valuable lifesaving drugs ever developed. In 1928 he noticed that his petri dish of staphylococcus bacteria had become contaminated with symmetrically growing, circular colonies of *P. notatum*. Around each speck, all the bacteria were dead. Fleming further found that the mould also killed pneumonia, gonorrhea and diphtheria germs – without harming human cells. The unassuming bluish-green mould was beginning to look more interesting, but Fleming could not isolate the active element. Not until 1939 did Howard Florey and Ernst Chain identify penicillin, a secretion of the growing mould, as the bacteria-killer. The first important antibiotic, penicillin revolutionised treatment of many diseases. Fleming, Florey and Chain won the Nobel Prize in Physiology/Medicine in 1945 for their pioneering work with the common fruit mould that yielded the first 'miracle drug'.

6. The Gourmet's Delight (*Penicillium roquefortii*)

According to an old legend, a French shepherd forgot his lunch in a cave near the town of Roquefort and when he found it weeks later, the cheese had become blue-veined and was richly flavoured. No one knew why this happened until American mycologists discovered the common blue mould *P. roquefortii* in 1918. All blue cheeses – English stilton, Italian gorgonzola, Norwegian gammelost, Greek kopanisti and Swiss paglia – derive their tangy flavour from the energetic blue mould that grows rapidly in the cheese, partially digesting it and eventually turning the entire cheese into mould. Of course, it's more appetising to say that *P. roquefortii* ripens the cheese instead of rotting it, but it's the same process.

7. The Famine-maker (*Phytophthona infestans*)

The political history of the world changed as a result of the unsavoury activity of *P. infestans*, a microscopically small fungus which reduced Ireland to desperate famine in 1845. Hot, rainy July weather provided perfect conditions for the white fungus to flourish on the green potato plants – most of

Ireland's food crop – and the bushes withered to brown, mouldy, stinking clumps within days. The entire crop was devastated, causing half a million people to starve to death, while nearly two million emigrated, mostly to the United States. *P. infestans* dusted a powdery white death over Ireland for six years. The fungus spread rapidly and just one bad potato could infect and ruin a barrel of sound ones. British Prime Minister Robert Peel tried to get Parliament to repeal tariffs on imported grain and while the MPs debated, Ireland starved. Relief came so slowly and inadequately that Peel's government toppled the next year, in 1846.

8. The Temperance Fighter (*Plasmopara viticola*)

A soft, downy mildew infecting American-grown grapes was responsible for nearly ruining the French wine industry. In 1872 the French unwittingly imported *P. viticola* on grafting stock of wine grapes grown in the United States. Within 10 years, the mild-mannered mildew had quietly decimated much of France's finest old vineyards. But in 1882 botanist Pierre-Marie-Alexis Millardet discovered a miraculous cure for the ravages of *P. viticola*. He noticed that Médoc farmers painted their grape leaves with an ugly paste of copper sulphate, lime and water – to prevent theft. Called Bordeaux mixture, this paste was the first modern fungicide. The vineyards of France recovered as the entire world sighed with relief.

9. Merchant of Death (*Saccharomyces cerevisiae*)

Ordinary brewers' yeast, *S. cerevisiae*, used to leaven bread and make ale, was once employed as a wartime agent of death. During WWI, the Germans ran short of both nitroglycerin and the fat used in its manufacture. Then they discovered that the usually friendly fungus *S. cerevisiae* could be used to produce glycerin, a necessary ingredient in explosives. Fermenting the fungus together with sucrose, nitrates, phosphates and sodium sulphite, the Germans produced more than 1,000 tons of glycerin per month. According to some military sources, this enabled them to keep their war effort going for an additional year.

10. The TB Killer (*Streptomyces griseus*)

A lowly mould found in dirt and manure piles, *S. griseus* nevertheless had its moment of glory in 1943, when Dr Selman Waksman discovered that it yields the antibiotic streptomycin, which can cure tuberculosis. Waksman went to the United States in 1910 as a Russian refugee and by 1918 he had earned his doctorate in soil microbiology. He had worked with *S. griseus* before, but not until a crash programme to develop antibiotics (a word coined by Dr Waksman himself) was launched did he perceive the humble mould's possibilities for greatness. Streptomycin was first used successfully on human beings in 1945, and in 1952 Dr Waksman was awarded the Nobel Prize in Physiology/Medicine.

– K.P.

10 Animals
That Have Eaten
Humans

1. Bears

The North American bear, although smaller and less aggressive than the grizzly, can be deadly and has been responsible for many harmful attacks on humans. In 1963, when the Alaskan blueberry crop was poor, hungry black bears attacked at least four people, one of whom they killed.

2. Crocodiles

Estuarine crocodiles are the most prolific man-eaters on Earth, killing approximately 2,000 people a year. On the night of February 19, 1945, they were responsible for the most devastating animal attack on human beings in recorded history. British troops had trapped 1,000 Japanese infantrymen, many of whom were wounded, in a swampy area in the Bay of Bengal. The noise of gunfire and the smell of blood attracted hundreds of crocodiles, and by evening the British could hear terrible screams. The following morning, only 20 Japanese were found alive.

3. Giant Squid

The giant squid is the most highly developed of the invertebrates. Its eyes are almost exact replicas of human eyes. It has 10 arms, and its body can reach up to 65 feet in length. Often confused with the octopus, which attacks humans only when threatened, the giant squid is a carnivorous predator. One notable incident occurred on March 25, 1941, when the British ship *Britannia* sank in the Atlantic Ocean. As a dozen survivors clung to their lifeboat, a giant squid reached its arms around the body of a man and pulled him below. Male squid sometimes eat the female after mating.

4. Komodo Dragon

The world's largest lizard, the Komodo dragon can reach 10 feet in length and weigh more than 300 pounds. They are the top predators on the handful of Indonesian islands where they live. Their prey normally consists of deer, wild goats and pigs, but they will eat anything they can catch, including the occasional human. Komodo dragons devour their prey completely, including the bones. All that was left of a French tourist killed in 1986 was his blood-stained shoes. All that was left of a German tourist eaten in 1988 was his mangled glasses.

5. Leopards

Considered one of the most dangerous animals to hunt, the leopard is quick and stealthy and is seldom observed. In the central provinces of India, leopards have been known to invade native huts to find their prey. One, known as the Panawar man-eater, is reputed to have killed 400 people. It was shot in 1910 by Jim Corbett, who also killed the Champawat man-eating tigress the following year.

6. Lions

Like tigers, lions do not usually attack humans. Man-eating lions usually hunt in prides, or groups, although occasionally single lions and pairs have become man-eaters. In October 1943, a lone lion was shot in the Kasama District of what is now Zambia after it had killed 40 people.

7. Puma (Mountain Lion)

Pumas have been known to catch prey seven to eight times their own size: a 100-lb female has been seen killing an 800-lb bull elk. In recent years, as people have built subdivisions in the mountains of the Western US, attacks by pumas on humans have exploded. Since 1970, there have been more than 40 attacks, at least 7 of them fatal. In 1994, two female joggers in California were killed and partly consumed by female pumas.

8. Python

Pythons are quite capable of killing people, and several such incidents have been reported since they became a trendy pet in the 1990s. However, most reports of pythons actually eating humans have proven untrue. A picture circulating on the internet of a boy allegedly recovered from a python's digestive tract is a hoax. However, there is at least one credible report. In 1992, a group of children playing in a mango plantation near Durban, South Africa, was attacked by a 20-foot rock python, which swallowed one of them. Craig Smith, the owner of a snake park, declared, 'I've dealt with a few cases like this and I always dispel them as absolute rubbish. But in my opinion this one did happen.'

9. Sharks

Of the 200 to 250 species of shark, only 18 are known to be dangerous to humans. The most notable are the great white, the mako, the tiger, the white-tipped, the Ganges River and the hammerhead. The best-known of all individual 'rogue' shark attacks occurred on July 12, 1916. Twelve-year-old

Lester Stilwell was swimming in Matawan Creek, New Jersey, 15 to 20 miles inland, when he was attacked by a great white shark. Both he and his would-be rescuer were killed. In 10 days four people were killed over a 60-mile stretch of the New Jersey coast. Two days after the last attack, an $8\frac{1}{2}$ foot great white was netted just 4 miles from the mouth of the creek. According to the Florida Museum of Natural History, between 1670 and 2003 there were 833 confirmed unprovoked shark attacks in the United States, 52 of which were fatal.

10. Tigers

A tigress known as the Champawat man-eater killed 438 people in the Himalayas in Nepal between 1903 and 1911. Tigers do not usually hunt humans, unless the animals are old, or injured, or have become accustomed to the taste of human flesh.

Note: AND TWO WHO WOULD NOT

While it is almost certain that wolves have preyed on human beings at some time in history, there are no confirmed reports of unprovoked attacks on humans by North American wolves. Likewise, there are no confirmed reports of piranha-caused deaths. Observers in the river regions of northeastern South America do report that many natives have lost fingers, toes or penny-sized chunks of flesh while bathing in piranha-infested waters. A school of piranhas can strip a wounded alligator of flesh in five minutes, but they are generally sluggish in their movements.

— D.L. & C.F.

THE BOOK OF LISTS: LONDON

Nick Rennison

Quirky, unexpected, revelatory – see London laid bare . . .

9 Unusual London Pub Names

5 Beastly Sites in London

12 Fictional Londoners

6 London Cross-Dressers

8 London Highwaymen

8 London Whores

9 London Gangsters

10 London Crime Statistics

6 Espionage Sites in London

With over 120 lists, in chapters covering every imaginable (and inconceivable) aspect of London, here is a fount of facts about this great city – which revolutionary Communist leader worked in a London hotel; how the River Fleet got lost; how Threadneedle Street got its name – and much more.

Every self-respecting Londoner needs this book.

£9.99 HBK

ISBN: 1 84195 676 7

THE BOOK OF LISTS: FOOTBALL

Stephen Foster

'An essential read for England fans everywhere . . . I guarantee you will find yourself quoting from this utter gem of a book.' *The Sun*

Featuring loads of this sort of thing . . .

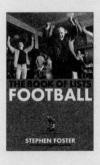

10 Compromising Positions

12 Swift P45s

Lard XI

10 Goalkeepers Who Have Scored

10 Tannoy Announcements

7 Existential Crises

7 Petty Regulations

11 Words of Wisdom

10 Reasons why the World Cup is Great

10 Reasons why the World Cup is Crap

'Some people think football is a matter of life and death. I am disappointed with that attitude. I can assure you it's much, much more important than that.' Bill Shankly

£8.99 PBK

ISBN: 1 84195 761 5

THE BOOK OF LISTS

David Wallechinsky and Amy Wallace

The internationally bestselling and dangerously compulsive reference book, packed with fascinating facts and bizarre stories.

10 Men Who Cried in Public

7 Almost Indestructible People

30 Achievers after the Age of 86

7 Famous People Expelled From School

10 Film Scenes Left on the Cutting Room Floor

The 7 Films In Which John Wayne Died

24 Strange Deaths

21 Stuffed or Embalmed Humans and Animals

The first and best compendium of facts weirder than fiction, of intriguing information and must-talk-about trivia has spawned many imitators – but none as addictive or successful.

'Impossible to put down.' *Independent on Sunday*
'Imaginatively insane.' *Sunday Herald*
'Oddly addictive.' *Sunday Express*

£7.99 ISBN: 1 84195 661 9